Merry Christmas to my love – I know
you'll enjoy this !

Dec. 25, 1996

Twin Cities
Then and Now

Twin Cities Then and Now

LARRY MILLETT

With New Photography
by Jerry Mathiason

Minnesota Historical Society Press • St. Paul

Publication of this book was supported, in part, with funds provided to the Minnesota Historical Society by the George A. MacPherson Fund, St. Paul.

Minnesota Historical Society Press
St. Paul 55102

This publication is printed on a coated paper manufactured on an acid-free base to ensure its long life.

Printed in Canada
10 9 8 7 6 5 4 3 2 1

International Standard Book Number
0-87351-326-6 Cloth
0-87351-327-4 Paper

Library of Congress Cataloging-in-Publication Data

Millett, Larry, 1947-
    Twin Cities then and now / Larry Millett ; with new photography by Jerry Mathiason.
        p. cm.
    Includes bibliographical references and index.
    ISBN 0-87351-326-6 (cloth). — ISBN 0-87351-327-4 (pbk.)
    1. Minneapolis (Minn.)—History—Pictorial works. 2. Minneapolis (Minn.)—Pictorial works. 3. Minneapolis (Minn.)—Social life and customs—Pictorial works. 4. Saint Paul (Minn.)—History—Pictorial works. 5. Saint Paul (Minn.)—Pictorial works. 6. Saint Paul (Minn.)—Social life and customs—Pictorial works. I. Title.
F614.M6M46 1996
977.6'579'00222—dc20   96-5746

Contents

To my children

Matthew

Molly

Alexandra

Corey

Acknowledgments

Writing history is always, to one degree or another, a joint enterprise, and there are many people who supported my work on *Twin Cities Then and Now*. My first note of thanks goes to Jerry Mathiason, who took the new black-and-white photographs that are integral to this book. Jerry was always a pleasure to work with and from the very start understood what I hoped to accomplish. And even though he often had to shoot under less than ideal conditions, he always found a way to capture the image that we needed.

Several of the new photographs for this book had to be taken from the upper floors of buildings in order to match historic views. Fortunately building owners and managers proved to be extremely accommodating when Jerry and I sought permission to record a bit of history from their property. Among those I wish to thank in Minneapolis are Roseanne Monten at Carmichael-Lynch, Inc.; Tim Oskey at the Loring Bar and Cafe; Surinder Singh at University Travel Services; and Paula Klimek at the La Rive Condominiums. In St. Paul, thanks go to Archie Gingold, owner of the old Forepaugh Building at Seven Corners; Marian Rose at Pioneer Vending; Dawn Horst at the Degree of Honor Building; Mary Alt and Thomas Roth-Yousey at the U.S. Postal Service; Scott Johnson at the Ashton Building; and Cheryl Rose and Patrick Sweeney at the St. Paul Cathedral. If I have forgotten the names of others who lent a hand in this regard, my deepest apologies.

Many other people assisted me along the way as I put this book together. John Mallander, an old friend, spent many days with me at the Minnesota Historical Society searching for suitable historic street scenes, and his help speeded this task enormously. John also undertook a variety of other research chores, including more than a few trips around the Twin Cities to find the current name or address of a building.

Among the others who aided me with this project, two people in particular deserve special mention. Paul Clifford Larson shared his matchless knowledge of Twin Cities architectural history by helping me identify and properly date numerous buildings that appear in this book. He also proved to be a source of last resort in cases where I could not find the architect of a particular building. In just about every instance, Paul came up with the name I needed. In addition, he read an early version of the manuscript and made many valuable suggestions, along with more than a few corrections, for which I am grateful.

I received assistance of a similar kind from James Sazevich, whom I regard as the official historian of St. Paul, even if that title has yet to be bestowed upon him. I am especially thankful for the information Jim provided regarding Payne Avenue, Twelfth Street, and the Upper Levee Flats—three of the many St. Paul places that fall within the vast realm of his expertise. He also read the manuscript and offered many pertinent insights.

Alan Lathrop, curator of the Northwest Architectural Archives at the University of Minnesota, was another source of help, providing answers to several knotty questions and lending his expert eye to the manuscript. Barbara Bezat, assistant at the archives, was also exceedingly accommodating when I made my periodic calls for assistance.

Many other librarians and historians also gave freely of their time and knowledge as I researched this book. In particular, I wish to thank Edward Kukla and his unfailingly cooperative staff at the Minneapolis Collection in the Minneapolis Public Library; Priscilla Farnham and her staff at the Ramsey County Historical Society; Dorothea Guiney at the Hennepin History Museum; Aaron Isaacs of the Minnesota Transportation Museum, who made his excellent collection of photographs available to me; the reference staff at the St. Paul Public Library; and the staff (including former chief librarian Linda James) at the library of the *St. Paul Pioneer Press*, where I have worked for nearly a quarter of a century. Unfortunately I was not permitted access to the library of the Minneapolis-based *Star Tribune*. My hope is that one day the newspaper will adopt a more enlightened and welcoming policy toward historic researchers.

At the Minnesota Historical Society, where much of my research was done, I am grateful to many people. Jean Brookins, assistant director for publications and research, and Deborah Miller, research supervisor, helped me obtain a research grant that was essential to the project. Ann Regan, managing editor of MHS Press, was an early and enthusiastic supporter of the book. So, too, was Al Ominsky, production supervisor, who provided advice on the selection of photographs and shepherded the book through the production process.

Also supportive at MHS were: Bonnie Wilson, curator of sound and visual collections, Jon Walstrom, map curator, and the staff of the Research Center and the Photo Lab.

My chief contact at the society was Sally Rubinstein, who has edited all three of my books published by the MHS Press. Sally did an especially fine job of putting together the often complicated pieces of this book, which at certain stages did indeed resemble the proverbial jigsaw puzzle. And even though Sally and I will never agree on the placement of commas, I consider myself fortunate to have worked with such a patient and capable editor.

Finally, I would like to thank my wife, Stacey, for all her support during the rather frantic months when this book came together.

Note to the Reader

The information boxes included with each then-and-now sequence provide the names, addresses, architects (if known), and construction dates of prominent buildings and places visible in photographs. If applicable, demolition dates (always preceded by a hyphen) are also given. Supplementary dates indicate when a building received a major addition, a new façade, or some other significant alteration. Similarly more than one demolition date indicates that a building was destroyed in stages. Numbers assigned to buildings or places in each box correspond to numbers located above or below the accompanying photographs. By looking straight up or down from the number, the reader will find the building or place in question. Finally in cases where a building or place has survived from the old to the new photograph, the same number is used to identify it in both.

Twin Cities
Then and Now

Time and Transformation

In 1891, Montgomery Schuyler, the foremost architecture critic of his day, paid a visit to Minneapolis and St. Paul. A few months later, he recorded his impressions in a long essay for *Harper's Magazine*. Schuyler found much to admire and more than a little to abhor in the exuberant architecture of the booming young cities. But he was especially struck by what he called their "electric air"—a wildly energetic atmosphere of growth and change "where antiquity means the day before yesterday, and posterity the day after to-morrow, the present is the most contemptible of tenses, and men inevitably come to think and live and build in the future-perfect."

The "electric air" noted by Schuyler has lost little of its galvanizing force over the past century. Growth and change continue to be dominant characteristics of the Twin Cities, so much so that many of the buildings and places visited by Schuyler a century ago are already long gone. Schuyler, in fact, would hardly recognize much of downtown St. Paul and Minneapolis today. Nor, for that matter, would someone familiar with the two downtowns just thirty years ago.

In this respect, the Twin Cities are not unique. Cities in general—and American cities in particular—are among the least stable of human creations. To observe a city over time is to see, for better or worse, the remorseless power of change. This is especially true in the case of buildings. Although architecture is often thought of as the most monumental and enduring of the arts, it is actually among the most fragile. Buildings come and go with blinding speed in American cities—a trend that is hardly new. As early as the 1880s, newspapers in the Twin Cities published nostalgic sketches of old monuments swept away by the powerful tide of progress. In other cases, there was barely time for nostalgia, as evidenced by the fate of a lavish bank constructed in downtown Minneapolis in 1906 (see page 50). The building stood for all of eight years before it was torn down to make room for a much larger replacement.

Yet there is one urban feature—the street system—that normally endures far longer than buildings. That is not to say streets are immutable. They can be widened, realigned, or even eliminated. St. Paul, which seems never to have liked its rather crooked and confusing layout, has been particularly energetic about street alterations. Minneapolis, on the other hand, has tended to leave its streets alone and concentrate instead on the destruction of old buildings. Nonetheless, it is fair to say that in both cities the vast majority of streets that existed, say, one hundred years ago follow the same course today, even though everything around them—from buildings and trees to stop signs and lampposts—may well have been replaced several times.

Because of their relative stability, streets offer an incomparable framework for looking at the urban past and comparing it with the present. Moreover, because photographers often shoot street scenes to illustrate their communities, a solid body of work exists that can be used for comparative purposes.

And so this book, which grew out of a seemingly simple idea: Select a varied group of historic Twin Cities street scenes and then shoot new photographs from the same locations, thereby showing the inevitable and sometimes astounding changes that have occurred over time. Yet this book proved to be far more difficult to put together than either I or photographer Jerry Mathiason could have imagined, and not only because Jerry sometimes had to climb to ridiculous places or brave the perils of downtown traffic in order to capture a particular scene.

The initial challenge was to choose the historic photographs, a responsibility that largely fell to me. I quickly discovered that there are literally thousands of old street scenes of the Twin Cities housed in local archives and that selecting a mere seventy-five or so nuggets from this rich lode of visual ore was a daunting task indeed. After examining as many of these images as I could, I found myself with more than five hundred "possibilities," all photocopied and indexed and begging for inclusion in the book. But over a long summer of looking, thinking, and winnowing, I was gradually able to develop a loose set of criteria that guided the final selection of the historic street scenes presented here.

First of all, I sought out old street scenes that are

lively and interesting. That meant pictures with something going on—with streetcars, wagons, automobiles, or other vehicles moving about, with pedestrians on the sidewalks, and with plenty of signs and other evidence of commercial vitality. As a result, many of the old photographs in this book will reward a close examination, for they are full of fascinating details from the past. Of course, not all the historic pictures meet this criterion, but most offer more than just a line of buildings receding into the distance. Street life in the Twin Cities was once far livelier than it is now, and the old photographs presented here generally demonstrate this fact.

Second, I tried to avoid the usual photographic suspects. Certain streets—Summit Avenue in St. Paul comes to mind—have been photographed extensively over the years, so much so that they have become almost overly familiar in their various historic manifestations. While readers will certainly find some well-known scenes here—there is a Nicollet Avenue then-and-now sequence, for example—they will also see images of infrequently photographed and rather out-of-the-way streets. In fact, a number of the historic photographs in this book have never, to my knowledge, been published before.

Third, I made a deliberate decision to avoid going too far back in time. The earliest images in this book are from the 1880s, which is when Minneapolis and St. Paul grew into major cities. There are no very old street views, say from the 1850s or 1860s. Looking at images from that pioneer era is a bit like looking at one's own baby pictures—the little creature giggling before the camera has great curiosity value but does not necessarily tell much about the adult whom he or she became. On the other hand, a picture taken at age thirteen may reveal an extraordinary amount about the later adult. So it is with the Twin Cities. While pre-1880s street scenes can indeed be captivating—they show, among other things, the raw landscape out of which the cities developed—I believe they are not especially useful for comparative purposes because so little remains of the urban world they depict. Therefore, the bulk of the historic photographs here are from the twentieth century, including

a substantial number taken as recently as the 1950s.

Fourth, I selected images that dramatize change. This inevitably led me to use a great many photographs from the downtown and near-downtown areas of Minneapolis and St. Paul. These old neighborhoods—with their offhand mix of commercial, residential, and institutional uses—offered some of the most varied and intriguing streetscapes in the Twin Cities. Unfortunately, they have been ravaged over the years by urban renewal, freeway construction, and other forms of "progress." The street scenes I have included from these downtown edge zones may well come as a revelation to younger readers. In many cases, it is simply hard to believe how dense and richly textured these neighborhoods were and how thoroughly they have been destroyed.

Fifth, I decided to limit the scope of this book to Minneapolis and St. Paul proper. The suburbs—especially the older ones with well-developed main streets—certainly offer some intriguing then-and-now sequences of their own. I found, however, that most comparative scenes from the suburbs would fall into the broad category of what I call cornfield-to-subdivision pictures. Rather than use just a few suburban photographs, which is probably all this book could have supported, I thought it would be wiser to concentrate on the central cities and leave the documentation of suburban change to other scholars.

My final criterion for selecting historic street scenes was practical in nature. Simply put, I looked for scenes that could be rephotographed in a way that would make visual sense to readers. This sounds like an obvious thing to do, but the fact is that some historic Twin Cities street scenes no longer exist in any recognizable form, and I saw no point in offering new views that might consist of little more than a blank wall or a clump of trees.

Take, for example, a fetching picture of St. Paul's Central Park, located just southeast of the State Capitol. Dating from around 1900, the photograph is really quite lovely, but trying to capture the same scene today, from anything like the same vantage point, would be futile. The problem is that a new photograph would show nothing except one end of the

Central Park, ca. 1900

large state parking ramp behind the Centennial Office Building that replaced Central Park in the 1960s.

Similar difficulties are presented by a delightful 1925 picture of Marshall Alley in St. Paul. The alley, which resembled a narrow, Old World lane and even had a sidewalk on one side, was just north of Marshall Avenue between Louis and Virginia Streets. Today, alas, this pleasant urban scene is utterly gone, buried within the campus of the St. Paul Technical College. A new photograph would offer only a scene of bland institutional corridors.

Or, from the post-World War II era, consider a 1954 picture looking south down La Salle Avenue at Thirteenth Street in Minneapolis, where the American Automobile Association maintained its

local headquarters (center). Today, the intersection, the AAA building, and everything around it have vanished, replaced in the 1970s by the Loring Greenway and an array of high-rise apartment buildings. Rephotography in this instance would yield only a close-up view of apartment balconies.

A few other points are worth mentioning about the nature and purpose of this book. To begin with, it is not a documentary project, which means I have made no attempt to offer a comprehensive, street-by-street or decade-by-decade look at the changing face of the Twin Cities. Such an undertaking would, in any event, be all but impossible because few if any streets in either Minneapolis or St. Paul have been photographed consistently from the same place over time.

In those rare cases where a sequence of pictures taken from the same vantage point is available, however, I have used as many photographs as possible to illustrate the evolution of that scene. One example is a sequence of four views of St. Paul's West Side Flats, taken over a span of more than sixty years from the same locale, Prescott Point.

Because I have sought out images of change, it is fair to say that this book presents a somewhat skewed view of past and present in the Twin Cities. It certainly would have been possible to select another set of images that showed less drastic transformations. There are, for example, numerous residential streets in the Twin Cities that have changed remarkably little since their initial development. Readers, in fact, may wonder why so few residential scenes are presented in this book. There are at least two reasons.

One is that residential views are not nearly as abundant in the historical archives as downtown and commercial street scenes, and so the pool of good photographs from which to draw is relatively small. There is also what I call the arboreal problem, which stems from the fact that residential streets in Minneapolis and St. Paul have been well planted with boulevard trees for over a century. Since most old residential scenes were shot during the summer months (photographers do not like to work in the deep freeze of a Minnesota winter any more than anyone else does), historic views often show little except a line of trees and a few houses peeking out from behind the greenery. Despite the ravages of Dutch elm disease, the urban forest remains a formidable visual element along most Twin Cities residential streets, with the result that modern comparative photographs do not yield especially interesting views.

The new photographs taken by Jerry Mathiason in the summer and fall of 1995 deserve some comment. When Jerry and I discussed the project, we agreed that our goal was not to achieve unerring exactitude in duplicating the angle, lighting conditions, and field of view of the historic photographs. A purist approach would have been futile in any case because of the many changes that have occurred in both cities over the years. Rather, our aim was to provide a good sec-

Marshall Alley, ca. 1925

La Salle at Thirteenth, 1954

ond look—one as close to the old view as possible, to be sure—but also one that would be interesting and visually pleasing in its own right.

Still, Jerry and I discovered that all manner of obstacles conspire to make the art of rephotography a demanding one. Often, our first challenge was simply to figure out where the earlier photographer had shot a particular scene. This task proved to be especially tricky in parts of St. Paul, where numerous streets—mainly in and around the downtown area—have been widened, moved, or vacated since the turn of the century. Usually, some straightforward detective work, such as consulting old atlases or carefully noting extant landmarks in historic pictures, yielded a reasonably accurate vantage point for the new photograph.

Other impediments to Jerry's work were more physical in character. The old views were shot from a wide variety of locations—rooftops, balconies, windows, and, of course, from the street. To replicate scenes, Jerry had to scramble up more than a few ladders (often using a special backpack to carry his bulky camera), squeeze through trapdoors, lean out windows, and, on one memorable occasion, climb a seemingly endless spiral staircase and then cross three high roof ridges to take a picture from a dormer near the base of the St. Paul Cathedral's gigantic dome. It was indeed interesting work, although as I clambered up and over the cathedral's roof with Jerry, it occurred to me that I might have enjoyed it more had I been twenty years younger.

Traffic also proved to be a notable hazard. Many of the old photographs were taken from the middle or near the middle of streets. Today, especially with the prevalence of high-speed, one-way traffic in downtown areas, trying to photograph from the middle of the street can be a quick ticket to the hospital or worse. Exercising his instinct for survival, Jerry therefore reshot most street-level scenes from near the sidewalk, sometimes using parked cars as a shield against onrushing traffic.

And now to a final point, which has to do with the value of a book such as this. The changes over time revealed in the seventy-two then-and-now sequences here will hardly come as a surprise to anyone familiar with American urban history. Virtually every American city has experienced continual alteration of its built environment, and in this respect Minneapolis and St. Paul are perfectly typical. Cities, as one urban observer has written, "devour buildings," which in our aggressively capitalist society are simply another consumer commodity. What is surprising is how many buildings in the Twin Cities have managed to survive for a century or more, particularly in residential neighborhoods.

If there is any lesson to be learned from this book, it is that cities, like the people who build and occupy them, need to maintain their sense of continuity. A walk through any historic neighborhood of Minneapolis or St. Paul can be an enriching experience because the buildings provide a palpable link with the past, which in turn gives meaning to the present. It is no coincidence, I think, that in this era of crazed acceleration and unraveling social structure, the so-called neotraditional town movement has taken root. People are looking for a renewed sense of community because they have begun to suspect that the world of cul-de-sacs and shopping malls sprawling out beyond the beltway is in some deep and fundamental respect deficient for human needs. It would be fatuous to argue that we should return to the past, but I believe there are valuable lessons to be learned from the old way of making cities. And even though many of the images in this book depict cruel transformations, they can also serve as a source of ideas about how to create better cities in the decades ahead.

Photographer's Note
Jerry Mathiason

One of the most compelling aspects of photography is its ability to record a moment in time with great detail, so I found the opportunity to work on a project that used photography's documentary capabilities exciting. This project pulled me back in time through the window of the archival photograph while I discovered present neighborhoods and places through the window of my view-camera groundglass.

Rephotographing Twin Cities sites seemed to be a simple proposition; I could look at the old photograph and know where to stand for the new photo. I soon discovered that, to find the original camera site, it was necessary to hold up the archival eight-by-ten-inch print and scan back and forth between the print and the actual site, comparing the relationships among existing buildings and moving around until the perspective of the old view matched the current view. If the present site had only one remaining building, the comparison was made from window to window or by correlating the angles of the roof lines as they receded toward the horizon. That angle changed as I moved left or right or front to back, so this method could be deceptive. In a few cases, I missed the location by a whole block and had to reshoot the scene. Many times, the spot could be found but was in the middle of a busy street, or the original was shot from the roof of a streetcar in the middle of the road. I could not safely reproduce those photos, but I did my best, peeking out from behind parked cars. In one case, I prepared the camera beforehand and then timed the traffic light and leaped into the road, setting up the camera, exposing the film, and jumping back before the next wave of cars arrived. For sites that had no buildings remaining, I had to key off buildings or other landmarks in the distance and then project an imaginary line to the current site. A surveyor would

have been able to pinpoint an exact location, but I needed only a close approximation to convey the sense of how dramatically the site had changed from the time of the original photograph.

We also decided to include as much of the street activity as possible. Normally when I do architectural photography I am not concerned with people and cars, just the building, but we wanted to maintain a feel for the street life whenever possible. It was a challenge to get good composition when I was photographing people in motion while using a camera that is fixed, with no viewfinder once the film is loaded.

The equipment that I used for the project is fairly straightforward. All the shots were done with an architectural view camera on a tripod, using individual film plates, so it was not possible to make a "grab" shot. The camera is a four-by-five-inch Sinar F2 with a set of lenses ranging from 65 mm to 210 mm. Most of the shots were done with a 90 mm or 135 mm lens. The camera is supported by a good-sized Gitzo tripod. For roof shots and shots that were at some distance from where I had parked my car, I loaded the monorail camera and the lenses, film, and filters in a custom-made frame pack so that this relatively heavy and clumsy camera equipment could be carried to the site and up ladders and over rooftops. All the new views were made on T-Max 400 film, developed in D-76 developer.

Minneapolis
Downtown

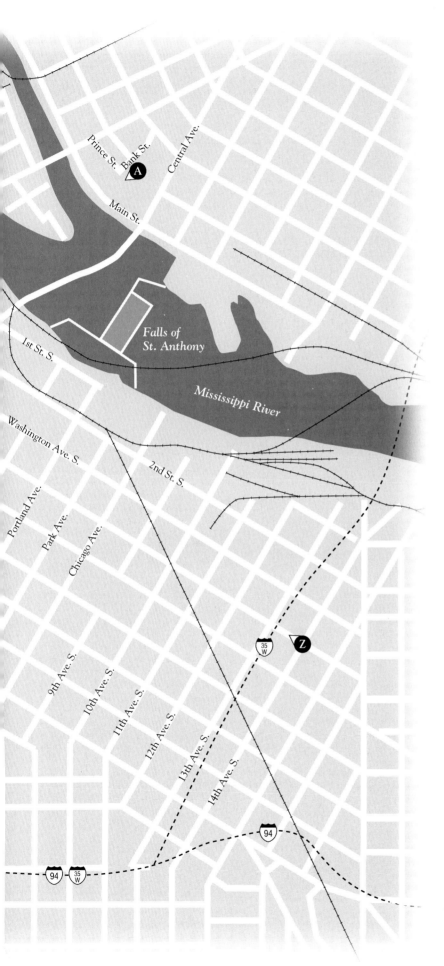

Minneapolis
Downtown

A. Nicollet Island and Downtown

B. Riverfront

C. Nicollet and Hennepin Avenues (The Gateway)

D. Washington Avenue

E. Nicollet Avenue, from Fourth Street

F. Nicollet Avenue, from Eighth Street

G. Third Street North

H. Fourth Street South

I. Fifth Street South

J. Fifth Street North

K. Sixth Street North

L. Seventh Street South

M. Hennepin Avenue

N. Eighth Street South

O. Tenth Street South

P. Marquette Avenue, from Ninth Street

Q. Marquette Avenue, from Fifth Street

R. Second Avenue and Fourth Street

S. Second Avenue South, from Tenth Street

T. Third Avenue South

U. Portland Avenue and Grant Street

V. Grant Street, from Spruce Place

W. Harmon Place

X. Loring Park

Y. Hennepin and Lyndale Avenues (The Bottleneck)

Z. Third Street South

This street map was drawn from a 1938 map of Minneapolis.

Nicollet Island and Downtown

West from Bank and Prince Streets, 1904

When the Industrial Exposition Building was constructed in southeast Minneapolis in 1886, it immediately became a magnet for photographers because of its 240-foot-high tower. Besides offering a superb vantage point for panoramic views of downtown, the tower came conveniently equipped with an elevator, which must have been a real boon for photographers loaded down with the heavy gear of that period.

This view, looking across the lower end of Nicollet Island, is especially fine because it captures downtown Minneapolis at the end of its first great age of develop-ment. Dominating the scene are a pair of massive structures—the Northwestern Guaranty Loan (soon to be renamed Metropolitan) Building and the Municipal Building (Minneapolis City Hall), its 345-foot-high tower then the tallest object on the downtown skyline. Around these two monuments are all manner of smaller structures, ranging from brick office blocks to churches to a scattering of old wood-frame houses still clustered near the river.

Also visible is the upper part of the Falls of St. Anthony, the natural feature that created Minneapolis and powered its flour mills for decades. The Mississippi at this time was strictly a working river (and a very polluted one at that), with railroad tracks and industrial buildings hugging its shoreline and nary a park in sight. Industry reliant on waterpower was also prominent on the lower end of Nicollet Island, where entrepreneur William W. Eastman in 1879 constructed the Island Power Building. The long, narrow stone structure—used by a variety of businesses—was notable for its resemblance to the much earlier factories of New England mill towns.

The Exposition Building came down in 1940, although the tower, shorn of its attached structure, survived until 1946. Today's view, taken at a somewhat wider angle than the earlier picture, was shot from a ninth-floor balcony of the La Rive Condominiums, which occupy part of the Exposition Building's site near Bank Street and Lourdes Place (formerly Prince Street).

The view has changed enormously since 1904. Esplanades instead of railroad tracks now parallel the river, the lower end of Nicollet Island is a park, and new bridges span the river. Meanwhile, the downtown skyline has grown a spectacular crop of modern skyscrapers, and only a handful of historic buildings—including the city hall and the Milwaukee Road Depot—have survived long enough to inhabit both photographs. There is no great surprise in this, since Minneapolis seems to consume its past with unusual gusto. It will be interesting, however, to see how long the proud towers that now populate the downtown skyline can withstand the city's appetite for change.

Buildings and Places

1. Municipal Building (Minneapolis City Hall), Fourth St. and Third Ave. S., Long and Kees, built 1889–1906
2. Milwaukee Road Depot, Washington and Third Ave. S., Charles S. Frost, 1898
3. Northwestern Guaranty Loan (later Metropolitan) Building, Third St. and Second Ave. S., 1890–1961
4. Island Power Building, Nicollet Island, 1879–ca. 1920s
5. Century Piano Co. (tower only visible), Prince St. and Bank St., Carl F. Struck, 1890–1917
6. Union Depot (train shed only visible), Hennepin and High St., 1885–1913
7. Third Avenue Bridge, 1916 (Frederick Cappelan), 1949, 1981
8. Federal Building and Courthouse (under construction and blocking view of city hall), Fourth St. and Fourth Ave. S., Kohn Pedersen Fox and The Alliance, to be completed 1996
9. U.S. Post Office (site of Union Depot), Hennepin and First St. S., 1933 (Magney and Tusler), ca. 1990 (Hammel, Green, and Abrahamson)
10. Hennepin Avenue Suspension Bridge, 1990

Riverfront

East across Hennepin Avenue from First Street and First Avenue North, ca. 1886–88

Sometimes the making of the new supplies a window on the old. Such is the case with these photographs, comparable views made possible in part by site clearance undertaken in 1994–95 for the new Minneapolis Federal Reserve Bank. The pictures provide a broad view across some of Minneapolis's most historic ground—a site at the foot of Hennepin Avenue that has gone through at least five generations of buildings since the founding of the city in 1855.

The old photograph is from one of Minneapolis's liveliest epochs—the 1880s—a period of phenomenal urban growth. Vigorous new businesses were erupting everywhere (the building advertising "Seeds," for example, was an early home of what later became the Northrup King Company), and new buildings sprang up with them. In fact, most of the buildings and structures visible here were quite recent at the time. The Union Depot had just opened in 1885, while the giant Industrial Exposition Building across the river was even newer. It was something of a marvel as well—it had taken only three months to build in 1886. The suspension bridge (the second on this site) was another structure of fairly recent vintage despite its quaint Gothic towers.

Note also the varied transportation systems on display here. At least two horsecars (electric trolleys were not introduced until 1890) can be seen on the bridge, along with a steady stream of wagons. In the foreground are two passenger trains powered by so-called "American type" (4-4-0) steam locomotives. The trains apparently are pos-

7   8   9

ing for the camera; otherwise, they would have been stopped beneath the depot's iron train shed (the arched structure next to the bridge tower).

Little from the old view except Our Lady of Lourdes Church survives today. The picturesque suspension bridge was gone by 1890, replaced by a more "modern" steel-arch bridge, which in turn gave way after a century of use to a rather squat new suspension span. The old depot also had a short life—it was torn down when the new Great Northern Depot opened on the other side of Hennepin. The Great Northern, of course, is itself only a memory now, and the new Federal Reserve Bank—a six hundred thousand square foot, $100 million colossus—is rising in its place after a heated preservation controversy over the demolition of five old buildings on the site. Whether the bank will prove to be an adornment to the city remains to be seen. What does seem certain is that it will not be the last building on a site that has already experienced plenty of architectural history.

Buildings and Places

1. Our Lady of Lourdes (originally First Universalist) Church, Lourdes Pl. near Bank St., 1857, ca. 1881, 1914
2. Industrial Exposition Building, Main St. and Central Ave., Isaac Hodgson, 1886–1940, 1946
3. Island Power Building, Nicollet Island, 1879–ca. 1920s
4. Hennepin Avenue Bridge (second), Thomas M. Griffith, 1876–89
5. Union Depot, Hennepin and High St., Hodgson and Son with James Brodie, 1885–1913
6. Northrup, Braslan & Goodwin Seed Co. Building, 10–12 Hennepin, ca. 1880–1907
7. Minneapolis Federal Reserve Bank (under construction), Hennepin and First St. N., Hellmuth, Obata & Kassabaum, to be completed 1997
8. Hennepin Avenue Bridge (fourth), Howard, Needles, Tammen, and Bergendoff, 1990
9. U.S. Post Office, Hennepin and First St. S., 1933, ca. 1990

Nicollet and Hennepin Avenues (The Gateway)

South from First Street, 1930

he Gateway, where Nicollet (left) and Hennepin come together, was for many years Minneapolis's "old town," a singular piece of the city drenched in history and alcohol. Never a particularly pretty place, it gradually devolved into skid row—home to flophouses, bars, liquor stores, pawn shops, cut-rate clothiers, and a floating population of (mostly) men living on the margin of life. Yet the Gateway also had a kind of dense, crumbling splendor, and no other part of the city could claim anything like its historic array of commercial buildings, some dating back as far as the 1860s.

Minneapolis, however, never sought to embrace the Gateway's historic riches for reasons that may have as much to do with the municipal psyche as anything else. By 1930 the Gateway had already become, in some peculiar sense, the city's unwelcome memory of itself, an irritating yet unshakable presence that seemed to sabotage long-held and deeply cherished notions of continual civic improvement. The Gateway, in other words, was a constant reproof to the very idea of progress.

This disgust with the Gateway—and its unfortunate denizens—helps to explain the ferocity with which it was attacked by the forces of urban renewal. Although renewal efforts began in 1915, when two blocks' worth of old buildings (including the first Minneapolis City Hall) were

cleared away for Gateway Park and its handsome pavilion, the main assault did not occur until the 1950s and 1960s. Funded by federal dollars, the city undertook a massive renewal project, and when the dust settled, the old Gateway was gone (except for the big flagpole, which was preserved only by moving it a bit to the northeast).

The modern view, shot from a slightly different angle, shows just how thorough the work of urban renewal was. Not a single building in the earlier photograph stands today, and the street pattern has been changed as well—Nicollet and Hennepin no longer meet. Among the residential and office high-rises that rose from the ruins, only the Northwestern National Life Insurance (now ReliaStar) Building, a lacy updating of the Parthenon, provides some measure of architectural grace. Even so, looking at the modern scene of wide streets and well-spaced buildings, you cannot help but feel that the real Gateway died long ago.

Buildings and Places

1. Nicollet (later Pick-Nicollet) Hotel, Hennepin and Washington, Holabird and Roche, 1924–91
2. Gateway Park and Pavilion, Hennepin and Washington, Hewitt and Brown, 1915–53 (pavilion), ca. 1960 (park)
3. Gateway flagpole, Nicollet and Hennepin, Daniel Chester French (sculptor of base), 1917, ca. 1960 (moved)
4. Gateway Building (originally Temple Court), Hennepin and Washington, E. Townsend Mix, 1886–1953
5. Pence Opera House, Second and Hennepin, Abraham Radcliffe, 1867, 1923–52
6. St. James Hotel, 12–14 Second St. N., ca. 1916–ca. 63
7. Towers Condominiums, 15–19 First St. S., John Pruyn, 1966
8. ReliaStar (formerly Northwestern National Life Insurance) Building, Washington at Nicollet, 1963
9. Rudy Luther Pontiac, Hennepin and Washington, ca. 1960s

Washington Avenue

East from near Nicollet Avenue, 1959

For much of its life, Washington Avenue in downtown Minneapolis presented two distinctive personalities. Southeast of Hennepin, Washington formed the core of the Gateway District, the Bowery of the Midwest, also known as "hobohemia." Northwest of Hennepin, however, Washington was, by the early years of this century, a street largely devoted to warehousing.

"Hobohemia" is long gone, swept away by the gigantic Gateway urban renewal project. Over the years, the Gateway project has acquired a bad odor, perhaps because its most notable excesses—such as the demolition of the Metropolitan Building in 1961–62—were so destructive of irreplaceable urban monuments. Yet scores of other, more modest buildings also disappeared as the city sought to scour away the last traces of blight in the Gateway.

The 1959 photograph, taken between Nicollet and Marquette Avenues, shows the old Gateway just before it vanished. Its defining architectural elements were small brick and stone buildings, two to four stories high and usually decked out with an array of garish signs. Preserved by alcohol (the many seedy bars and their customers discouraged upscale development), these buildings formed the

finest collection of nineteenth-century commercial architecture remaining in the Twin Cities at midcentury. The best of them, renovated and restored, could easily have been the basis for long-term renewal of the district.

It did not happen that way, as the 1995 photograph reveals. Instead, the old Gateway was simply leveled. What rose in its place was a world of isolated towers, large plazas, and acres of ornamental shrubbery. This new Washington Avenue South is certainly cleaner, more rational, and perhaps even safer than the old. But it is also much less alive and, from a purely visual perspective, much less interesting.

Change has been less dramatic along Washington Avenue North, as shown by a 1927 photograph taken from the Nicollet (later Pick-Nicollet) Hotel. Massive warehouses already dominated the avenue at this time. Many of these structures have since been converted to new uses, thereby helping to ensure their survival. A nonwarehouse building of note is also visible: the old Bijou Opera House, which on August 3, 1896, became the first theater in the Twin Cities to show a movie. Unfortunately, a contemporary view up Washington Avenue from the same lofty vantage point is all but impossible because the Nicollet Hotel was demolished in 1991 and the site remained a parking lot as of 1995.

8   9   *1927*

Nicollet Avenue

North from Fourth Street, ca. 1922
North from near Eighth Street, 1947

Probably no street in Minneapolis has been photographed more frequently than Nicollet Avenue. For well over one hundred years, Nicollet has been the heart of the downtown shopping district, and so many changes have occurred along its course that it could well be the subject of its own photographic documentary. These two historic views give only a small sampling of the street's evolution before it was transformed into the Nicollet Mall.

The first shopping district in Minneapolis was along Washington Avenue, but by the 1880s the retail core had begun to move south. A key event in this regard was the opening of Donaldson's Glass Block—the first modern department store in Minneapolis—at Sixth and Nicollet in 1888. Dayton's soon followed at Seventh and Nicollet, and other stores began to cluster around what became downtown's "100 percent" intersection (the one with the costliest real estate).

By the early 1920s, lower Nicollet had become something of a cut-rate shopping area, with numerous small-to medium-sized clothing stores. The buildings along the street date mostly from the 1880s and show the usual

1   2   3   4   5   *Ca. 1922*

range of Victorian styles. Especially handsome is the small Gothic building at left that housed Sorenson Shoes beneath a marvelously literal sign. Directly across from the shoe store is the Renaissance-revival style Wood Block, which featured modish balconies and a rooftop clock. The building, home at this time to Maurice Rothschild and Company's clothing store, was notable for the fact that when it was built in 1882 it offered an unusual amenity: a gas-powered elevator.

The tallest building on the left is the old Bank of Minneapolis (by 1922 known as the Lincoln Building). This sophisticated seven-story office building, constructed in 1887, used metal-framing techniques every bit as advanced as those in Chicago. Farther down the street is the oldest building in the photograph—the Nicollet House Hotel, built in 1858 and expanded many times. Terminating the view is the Great Northern Railway Station, long a Minneapolis landmark.

The lack of traffic and small number of pedestrians suggest that this picture was made on a Sunday. The 1947 view of Nicollet, taken four blocks to the south between Eighth and Ninth, shows a much livelier scene. The period immediately following World War II brought huge crowds downtown, ready to shop and be entertained after years of wartime rationing and blackouts. Retailers responded by enlarging their stores. Dayton's, for example, was just finishing another addition to its flagship store at the time of this photograph (the addition is at left, with the temporary protective canopy over the sidewalk).

The boom times did not last for downtown, and by the mid-1950s suburban shopping malls such as Southdale were beginning to threaten Nicollet's retail hegemony. The city's response was to turn Nicollet into a mall in the 1960s in hopes of keeping shoppers downtown. Designed by Lawrence Halprin and Associates, the original mall, with its winding bus-way, had a certain loopy charm and proved to be quite successful. However, the mall was completely rebuilt in 1990–91 in a rather flat, formal style lacking the visual panache of its predecessor.

Despite its design deficiencies, the Nicollet Mall remains a significant contributor to downtown's well-being, and the view from Eighth today reveals that this

1947

9

10

11

part of Nicollet still enjoys a vibrant commercial life. Numerous new buildings have appeared since 1947, but most manage to accommodate street-level retailing, thus preserving Nicollet's status as the city's chief shopping venue. Although the Conservatory has fared so poorly that it is threatened with demolition, other retailing continues to flourish nearby. Dayton's still anchors the block between Seventh and Eighth across from the IDS Center, while farther down the mall newer developments such as Gaviidae Commons maintain Nicollet's strong retail tradition.

The contemporary view from Fourth and Nicollet is far less pleasing, however, and can only be described as a vision of emptiness. Everything from the 1922 photograph is gone, and lower Nicollet now extends through a vast vacancy of plazas and parking lots. It almost seems, in fact, that the city has simply disappeared, replaced by alien invaders from the overly spacious world of the suburbs. The Gateway project was largely responsible for this fiasco. It is unlikely that lower Nicollet will ever again achieve the rich urbanity it offered sixty years ago.

Buildings and Places

1. Gothic-style building, Nicollet near Fourth, ca. 1880–ca. 1958
2. Bank of Minneapolis (later Lincoln Building), Third and Nicollet, Hodgson and Son, 1887–ca. 1958
3. Nicollet House Hotel, Washington between Nicollet and Hennepin, 1858, ca. 1870–1923
4. Great Northern Station, Hennepin at Mississippi River, Charles S. Frost, 1914–78
5. Wood Block, 319–321 Nicollet, J. K. Wilson, 1882–ca. 1960
6. Minneapolis Public Library (site of Bank of Minneapolis), Fourth and Nicollet, McEnary and Kraft, 1959
7. ReliaStar (formerly Northwestern National Life Insurance) Building, Washington at Nicollet, 1963
8. Federal Reserve Bank, Marquette at Third, Gunnar Birkerts and Associates, 1973
9. Dayton's Department Store, Nicollet between Seventh and Eighth, 1902 (Charles Sedgwick), 1937, 1947 (Larson and McLaren)
10. Donaldson's Department Store and building, Nicollet between Sixth and Seventh, 1888 (Long and Kees), 1903, 1910, 1924 (Kees and Colburn), 1947–82
11. John W. Thomas & Co. Building, Eighth and Nicollet, Harry Jones, 1912–ca. 70
12. The Conservatory, Nicollet between Eighth and Ninth, BRW Architects, 1987
13. IDS Center, Seventh and Nicollet, 1973

Third Street North

West from Hennepin Avenue, ca. 1908

One of the ironies of development in most American cities is that buildings with some pretense to high style—ornate public piles, grandiose skyscrapers, sumptuous mansions—often live shorter lives than their more modest, working-class cousins. This is certainly true in Minneapolis, where innumerable fashionable monuments have come and gone while the city's no-nonsense warehouses of the late nineteenth and early twentieth century continue to adapt and thrive. With their rugged timber, iron, or concrete-frame construction and open loft floors, these warehouses lend themselves to an almost endless variety of new uses—as housing, offices, theaters, restaurants, or artists' studios, to name but a few adaptations.

To be sure, many old warehouses have disappeared over time in downtown Minneapolis, as these views along Third Street North demonstrate. Yet the photographs also reveal how much has remained in place over a span of nearly ninety years—a circumstance that exists along few streets in downtown Minneapolis except for those in the warehouse district.

The rather fuzzy view from about 1908 gives a sense of how plain, yet stately, the warehouse district was at the turn of the century. Although the buildings present a range of styles and date anywhere from the early 1880s to just after 1900, they seem all of a piece—solid citizens of commerce going about their business with a minimum of fuss

and bother. The many wagons in view and the crates piled up on the sidewalk underscore the fact that this was a hard-working part of the city. The tavern at lower right suggests hard drinking may have been part of the equation as well. But there is also evidence of nobler aspirations—the steeple of the Church of the Immaculate Conception, a landmark from the 1870s that was soon to vanish before the push of progress.

The 1995 view shows that the old buildings adjacent to Hennepin are gone, replaced by the inevitable parking lots. The street itself has also changed and is now a one-way artery feeding into Interstate 94. Farther down Third, however, many historic warehouses remain, although a few have lost their cornices or even a floor or two. Third today is not a beautiful street (it never was), but it remains more than respectable. It is a street that has managed to evolve into the present without shedding all traces of the past.

Buildings and Places

1. Boston Block, Third and Hennepin, 1882, 1887–1942
2. George R. Newell Co. Building (now 300 First Avenue North), Third St. and First Ave. N., 1887 (William H. Dennis), 1985
3. F. C. Hayer Building (now Traffic Zone Center for Visual Art), Third St. and Third Ave. N., Joseph Haley, 1886
4. Church of the Immaculate Conception, Third St. and Third Ave. N., Alden and Howe, 1872–ca. 1918
5. Harrison Block (now Minnesota Center for Book Arts), Third St. and First Ave. N., Warren H. Hayes, 1893
6. North Star Boot and Shoe Co., Third St. N. between Hennepin and First Ave. N., Warren H. Hayes, 1888, 1892–ca. 1975

Fourth Street South

West from near Nicollet Avenue, ca. 1900

The woman with the umbrella shading herself from the midday sun is walking along what was once one of the most delightful streets in Minneapolis. Before various forms of redevelopment began in the 1950s, Fourth Street offered an exceptionally rich collection of buildings to tempt the passing eye. And while the street was not exactly tidy—note the array of signs and miscellaneous bric-a-brac—its vitality is self-evident.

Among the prominent buildings is the Vendome Hotel (its sign is visible just behind the woman), a frothy French confection topped by a replica of the Statue of Liberty's head. Farther down the street, at Hennepin, is the old Kasota Block, a muscular essay in Richardsonian Romanesque. But by far the most intriguing building in sight is Spectator Terrace. Built by the eccentric publisher of a short-lived newspaper called the *Saturday Spectator*, the building was an architectural salmagundi whose unlikely ingredients included the rooftop pagoda visible here. (The rear of the building offered even more skyline madness in the form of an onion-shaped dome.)

Just a block away was perhaps the best-known section of Fourth Street—"Newspaper Row." Here, on the south side of the street between Nicollet and Hennepin, the ink-stained wretches of the Fourth Estate in Minneapolis conducted their business for many years. In this 1927 view, the city's two big dailies—the *Tribune* and the *Journal*—seem engaged in a battle to see which could mount the larger sign. The *Journal* appears to have won the battle, but it lost the war. Today the newspaper is only a memory, as is its building. The historic Tribune Building (later combined with an adjoining structure and renamed the Times Building) is also gone.

Today whatever charms Fourth Street once possessed have vanished. A parking ramp and the Northern States Power Company Building (not visible here) have long since replaced the Vendome Hotel and its handsome Victorian companions. This stretch of Fourth is now just another anonymous conduit for cars and certainly not the sort of street where a woman with a parasol might enjoy a stroll in the sun.

Buildings and Places

1. Vendome Hotel, 19–23 Fourth St. S., William H. Dennis, 1885–1960
2. Spectator Terrace (later Northwestern Fire and Marine Insurance Co.), 13–15 Fourth St. N., Alexander Murrie, 1889–ca. 1920
3. Wyman Building, First Ave. and Fourth St. N., Long and Kees, 1896
4. Kasota Block, Fourth and Hennepin, 1884 (Franklin B. Long), 1887, 1893 (Long and Kees)–1960
5. Tribune Building, Fourth and Nicollet, Long and Kees, 1899–1992
6. Journal Building, 47–49 Fourth St. S., William H. Dennis, 1890–1941
7. Midtown parking ramp (site of Vendome Hotel), Fourth between Nicollet and Hennepin, ca. 1967
8. Commercial building (site of Spectator Terrace), Fourth and Hennepin, 1920

5   6   *Ca. 1927*

7   8   3

Fifth Street South

East from near Nicollet Avenue, ca. 1947

Although it is customary to think of downtown Minneapolis as a place of rapid and continual transformation, there was a long period, from the turn of the century until about 1960, when the pace of change was actually quite gradual. A Minneapolitan familiar with downtown in 1915, for example, would have recognized most of the buildings in the 1947 view down Fifth Street. But the 1995 photograph would be disorienting, since it shows the impact of two modern build-

ing booms—the most recent in the 1980s—that have given a new look to much of downtown.

Almost all of the buildings in the historic view date from 1915 or earlier. The exception is the art-deco Northwestern Bell (later US West) Telephone Company Building, completed in 1931. Otherwise this scene—with its well-defined street wall of masonry buildings—has a decidedly old-fashioned look.

The oldest structure visible is the Syndicate Block, which was the city's largest commercial building when it opened in 1883. The Syndicate survived many lives, many looks, and at least one major fire over the years, but it is best remembered as the longtime home of the J. C. Penney Company, which in 1959 wrapped the building in an unflattering metal façade.

In 1947, however, Penney's was still across the street in

6   2   3   7   5

the old Andrus Building—itself something of a historic curiosity, since it was built in 1898 over and around an 1880s brick building known as the Sidle Block (whose developer, H. G. Sidle, once lived in a house on the site but moved it away when he saw the chance to make more money from the land). Another familiar Minneapolis retail institution—the Powers Department Store—is also prominent in this photograph.

Only bits and pieces remain of the Fifth Street of fifty years ago. The phone company building still stands but is obscured by a modern skyscraper. The Soo Line Building also survives, as does the Andrus Building, which was remodeled and rechristened Renaissance Square in the early 1980s. What is also noticeable is how much definition the street has lost, especially on the north side where the demolition of the Powers store has left a gaping hole.

Buildings and Places

1. Powers (originally S. E. Olson) Department Store, Fifth and Nicollet, 1893 (William H. Dennis), ca. 1910–92
2. Northwestern Bell (now US West) Telephone Co., Fifth St. and Third Ave. S., Hewitt and Brown, 1931
3. Soo Line Building (originally included First National Bank), Fifth and Marquette, Robert W. Gibson, 1914
4. Syndicate Block (later J. C. Penney store), Nicollet between Fifth and Sixth, 1883 (Kees and Fisk), ca. 1915, 1959–89
5. Andrus Building (now Renaissance Square), Fifth and Nicollet, 1898 (Long and Long), 1983
6. One Hundred South Fifth Street, Fifth and Marquette, Hellmuth, Obata & Kassabaum, 1985, 1988
7. Neiman Marcus Department Store (site of Syndicate Block), Fifth and Nicollet, Lohan Associates, 1991

Fifth Street North

North from Sixth Avenue North, 1958

The area immediately north of downtown Minneapolis has never been one of the city's favored precincts. Its generally flat terrain, lack of natural amenities (such as the lakes and hills to the south of downtown), and easy access to railroads made it a logical location for industry, and that has been its primary use for more than a century. Working-class housing was also a part of the area's mix at one time, but as industry pushed farther north, most of the housing gradually vanished (although many old buildings have now been converted to housing in the historic warehouse district nearby).

Yet Fifth Street's nondescript appearance in this vicinity has conferred upon it a measure of protection not afforded more desirable urban locales. With few distinctive natural or architectural features to recommend it, this resolutely unglamourous stretch of Fifth simply has not attracted much attention, and so no one has tried to redevelop it in any overwhelming way. As a result, these three views, extending over a period of sixty-five years, convey a surprisingly similar look and feel.

To be sure, there have been significant changes. The biggest transformation is not visible, for just out of view to the left in the new photograph is the immense Hennepin County garbage incinerator, a waste-burning colossus that has generated huge clouds of steam and controversy since its opening in 1989. Another modern addition—the offices and garage of the Metropolitan Council Transit Operations (MCTO)—can be seen along Sixth Avenue at far left in the 1995 view.

Several major deletions are also apparent. The streetcar tracks that lend a curving rhythm to the 1930 picture were already a thing of the past by 1958. Gone by 1995 was St. Joseph's Catholic Church, once the ecclesiastical anchor of a large working-class neighborhood. The church's twin octagonal spires appear in both old photographs (although they are barely visible in the 1930 view). A summer windstorm in 1967 destroyed these lovely old spires, and the church itself was demolished nine years later. Another significant building visible in both historic scenes, the Regan Brothers (later Holsum) Bakery, was also a casualty of progress by 1995.

Otherwise these photographs depict an urban backwater that over sixty-five years has managed to maintain much the same character. Two gas stations, for example, still face each other across the intersection at Sixth Avenue, just as they did in 1930. Even the tiny diner next to the Mobil station in the 1958 picture continues to hold its ground, an improbable resister to the powerful pressures of urban change.

1930 **1** **2**

Buildings and Places

1. Regan Brothers Bakery (later Holsum Bread Co.), 631–643 Fifth St. N., Edward S. Stebbins, ca. 1896–ca. 1980

2. Commercial building, Fifth St. near Sixth Ave. N., ca. 1900

3. St. Joseph's Catholic Church, Fourth St. and Twelfth Ave. N., Carl F. Struck, 1886–1976

4. MCTO offices and garage, 560 Sixth Ave. N., Setter, Leach and Lindstrom, 1986

1   2   3

4   2

Sixth Street North

West from near Second Avenue North, 1902

Municipal markets, where fresh produce from the countryside is sold to the hungry masses, have always been a lively feature of urban life. But the city markets of today in Minneapolis and St. Paul are much smaller and less colorful places than they used to be, as this delightful photograph attests.

The market building at left was actually the fourth in Minneapolis, which by 1902 was one of the nation's largest distributors of fresh produce. The city's original public market, where hay was a major product, developed in ad-hoc fashion in the 1860s around Bridge Square at the foot of Hennepin Avenue. It was not until 1869 that developer

Harlow Gale built the first city market building nearby. Then, in 1876, Gale erected a far more substantial market hall at First and Hennepin.

Unfortunately this location gradually proved to be un-workable, causing traffic snarls at what was already one of the city's "central and commanding corners," according to the *Minneapolis Journal*. In 1892, Gale and other investors

1

2   3

constructed a new central market on the block bounded by Sixth and Seventh Streets and Second and Third Avenues North. The building burned not long afterward, however, and had to be rebuilt on the same site in 1894.

This atmospheric photograph—you can almost smell what must have been a fragrant mix of food, horses, and manure—shows the market on a busy day. Wagons filled with bags and baskets of produce line up on either side of the street, while their owners have presumably gone inside to attend to business. Open-air sheds, where produce was sold to the public, were to the rear of the market building, as was a hotel. Wholesalers also bought large amounts of produce to be shipped out for resale.

The market was located here until the 1930s, when it became the site of a seminal event in Minneapolis history—the bloody clash on May 21, 1934, between striking teamsters and special deputies hired by Minneapolis businessmen. Only four years after this fabled confrontation, the Sixth Street market was gone, moved by the city to a new site on cleared land near Lyndale and Glenwood Avenues, where it remains today.

The 1995 photograph, taken from a point just west of First Avenue North, reveals that all traces of the old market building and its historic environs are gone. Interstate 394 now runs between Second and Third Avenues North, while the block just east of the old market hall is occupied by Target Center, a garish and overweening structure that has won few admirers. Progress has not been a complete disaster, however, for also visible here is Harry Jones's masterful Butler Brothers warehouse, constructed in 1907, twice renovated, and one of the undisputed treasures of Minneapolis architecture.

Seventh Street South

West from near Nicollet Avenue, ca. 1913

Although Hennepin Avenue was home to most downtown theaters in Minneapolis, Seventh Street could boast of a theatrical row of its own at one time. Four major theaters, which went by a variety of names over the years, were once located on Seventh within a block of Hennepin, making the street a

kind of entertainment annex. Like Hennepin, Seventh between Nicollet and First Avenue North was also a wonderfully varied street. It offered small shops, office buildings, hotels (including the popular Radisson), restaurants, and Dayton's big department store at Nicollet.

The view from about 1913, taken near Nicollet and looking west toward Hennepin, shows a corner of Dayton's as well as the Radisson, which was brand new in 1909 and was considered the city's grandest hotel. Just past the Radisson is the Orpheum Theater (not to be confused with the Orpheum on Hennepin). Later known as the Seventh Street Theater, the first Orpheum had eighteen hundred seats and was probably the city's largest theater when it

1   2   3   4   5   6   7   *Ca. 1913*

opened in 1904 as a vaudeville house. Visible on the north side of the street are two other theaters—the Strand and the New Garrick.

This photograph also demonstrates how automobiles, even at so early a date, were exerting tremendous pressures on cities like Minneapolis. Automobile parking was a particularly novel and difficult problem, and the city tried a variety of techniques, such as the center-of-the-street parking seen here. This kind of parking, today found only in a few small towns with very wide streets, was possible because Seventh had no streetcar tracks between Nicollet and Hennepin. Even so, the middle-of-the-road parking experiment did not last long, and parallel parking at the curb soon became the customary arrangement on Seventh and everywhere else downtown.

Another photograph from 1913 presents an exceptionally crisp view of Seventh, looking west across the intersection of Hennepin. The less-than-elegant Hotel Garrick holds down one corner, while farther down Seventh on the right is the Shubert (later Academy) Theater. Punctuating the skyline at left is the tall, saddle-roofed tower of the soon-to-be-demolished Jefferson School. Note also the many different modes of transportation visible—streetcar, automobile, bicycle, horse-drawn wagon, and, of course, old-fashioned foot power.

Like other downtown streets, Seventh evolved signifi-

4   8   *1913*

cantly in later years. Yet by 1950—as a photograph looking east from Hennepin reveals—Seventh still maintained much of its traditional character. The Strand Theater had by this time become the Forum Cafeteria, a popular eatery perhaps better known for its gleaming art-deco decor than for its food. Nearby, the New Garrick Theater, which became the Century in 1932, advertises a Joel McCrea movie, *Stars in My Crown*. The Century would soon become the downtown showplace for the new wide-screen Cinerama process, which premiered in 1952 with an in-your-face roller coaster sequence still remembered by anyone who saw it as a child.

Note also how busy this 1950 street scene is. The immediate postwar era was a prosperous period for downtowns everywhere in America, and it would be another decade or so before suburban malls and other developments began to take their toll on the old urban order.

The 1995 view west on Seventh from Nicollet shows that the street has assumed almost an entirely new look

since 1950, including the inevitable addition of skyway bridges. Only the Dayton's store, which retains its original 1902 façades, offers anything in the way of urban continuity. Not surprisingly, the theaters are long gone, except for the vacant hulk of the Shubert, only its name having been restored. The Forum closed in 1976, although much of its interior was saved and remounted, not entirely successfully, in a new restaurant.

On the north side of Seventh between Nicollet and Hennepin, everything was swallowed up in the early 1980s by the huge City Center–Marriott Hotel complex, which cannot be accounted as one of the city's architectural jewels. Shortly thereafter, the old Radisson across the street gave way to the Radisson Plaza Hotel, another indifferent piece of design. Despite such architectural failures, this section of Seventh—with its two big hotels, the perpetual lure of Dayton's, and the First Avenue nightclub just a block away—remains one of the livelier streets in downtown Minneapolis.

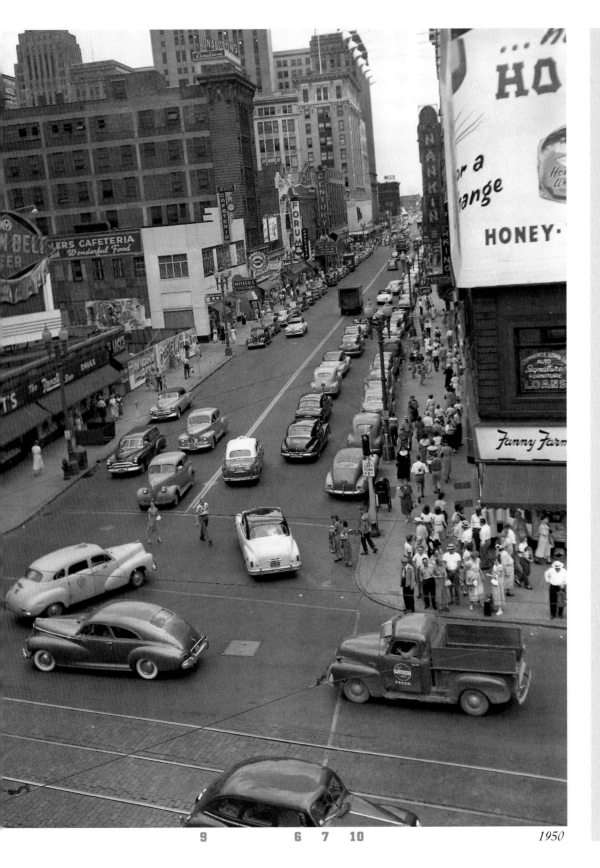

9   6 7 10   *1950*

Buildings and Places

1. Dayton's Department Store, Seventh and Nicollet, 1902
2. Radisson Hotel, 41–43 Seventh St. S., 1909 (Long, Lamoreaux, and Long), ca. 1960–82
3. Orpheum (later Seventh Street) Theater, 25 Seventh St. S., Kees and Colburn, 1904–39
4. Jefferson School, Seventh St. and First Ave. N., LeRoy S. Buffington, 1877–1914
5. Minneapolis Gas Light Co., 16–24 Seventh St. S., Long and Long, 1903–ca. 30s (temple-style building); 1910–ca. 70 (seven-story building)
6. Strand Theater (later Forum Cafeteria), 36 Seventh St. S., 1914, 1930 (George B. Franklin, Magney and Tusler)–79
7. New Garrick (later Century) Theater, 40 Seventh St. S., Kees and Colburn, 1907, 1910–65
8. Shubert (later Academy) Theater, 10–22 Seventh St. N., W. A. Swasey, 1910
9. Miller's Cafeteria, 20 Seventh St. S., 1876, ca. 1935–64
10. Donaldson's Department Store, Seventh and Nicollet, 1910–82
11. Radisson Plaza Hotel, 35 Seventh St. S., WZMH Group with Hammel, Green, and Abrahamson, 1987
12. Marriott Hotel and City Center, Seventh between Hennepin and Nicollet, Skidmore, Owings, and Merrill, 1982

Hennepin Avenue

North from near Seventh Street, 1937

Hennepin Avenue has long been the street where Minneapolis went to be entertained and even seek out a little sin, something not always easy to find in the generally sober Midwest. During its prime, the avenue was home to many theaters, and their names still form a familiar litany of amusement—the Orpheum, the State, the Pantages, the Lyric, the Grand, the Astor, and the Palace, among others. All told, Hennepin had at least ten movie theaters in 1937, mostly clustered between Sixth and Ninth. In addition, the avenue offered an array of cafés, grocery stores, clothing stores, nightclubs, and striptease joints, making it the city's most varied commercial street.

Hennepin was also an avenue of spirited and memorable architecture. Grand old hotels like the West, fanciful club buildings like the Masonic Temple, and stately office structures from the turn of the century (and even earlier) combined to create the walls of an outdoor recreation room that extended for a mile through the heart of downtown.

The 1937 view, looking north toward Sixth Street, shows Hennepin at its liveliest on an early June day. Automobiles, trucks, and a Como–Harriet streetcar vie for space on the street, a bicyclist threads his way through traffic, and people crowd the sidewalks. Meanwhile, the avenue's unruly collection of signs offer their usual blandishments, displaying capitalist clutter at its most endearingly vulgar.

Another photograph, from about 1940, shows the view south along Hennepin from between Sixth and Seventh. By this time, the Grand Theater had a new name (the Gopher) and a new art-deco marquee. Several other theaters—the Lyric, Pantages, and State—are also visible, as is the old Minneapolis Public Library, a rock-ribbed castle of culture that marked the end of Hennepin's entertainment corridor at Tenth.

One curiosity in the 1940 view is the crowd gathered around the automobile at the intersection of Seventh and Hennepin (right center). Had there been an accident? Was a body lying in the street? Was some street hustler giving the citizenry a lesson in three-card monte? The photograph does not tell, but clearly something or someone was drawing a crowd—and backing up traffic in the process.

Another picture, taken in 1927 and looking south from the top of the Nicollet Hotel at Hennepin and Washington, provides an exceptional view of the avenue's architecture. The north side of Hennepin was an especially rich landscape of nineteenth-century commercial buildings, including such landmarks as the Boston Block at Third, the Kasota Block at Fourth, and the West Hotel at Fifth. Newer structures such as the Andrews Hotel and the Plymouth Building can also be seen, and together these muscular masonry buildings give the avenue a genuine sense of grandeur.

1937   13   1   2   3   14

Buildings and Places

1. Masonic Temple (now Hennepin Center for the Arts), Fifth and Hennepin, Long and Kees, 1889
2. Lumber Exchange, Fifth and Hennepin, Long and Kees, 1886, 1891
3. Plymouth Building, Sixth and Hennepin, Long, Lamoreaux, and Long, 1910
4. Grand (later Gopher) Theater, 619 Hennepin Ave., ca. 1910, 1938 (Liebenberg and Kaplan)–ca. 80
5. Lyric (originally Blue Mouse) Theater, Hennepin between Seventh and Eighth, ca. 1910, 1923–ca. 70
6. State Theater, 805 Hennepin Ave., 1921 (J. E. O. Pridmore), 1991
7. Minneapolis Public Library, Tenth and Hennepin, Long and Kees, 1889–1961
8. Andrews Hotel, Fourth and Hennepin, 1911, ca. 1915–84
9. West Hotel, Fifth and Hennepin, LeRoy S. Buffington, 1884–1940
10. Kasota Block, Fourth and Hennepin, 1884, 1887–1960
11. Boston Block, Third and Hennepin, LeRoy S. Buffington, 1882, 1887–1942
12. Seymour Hotel (originally Sykes Block), 254 Hennepin, Warren H. Hayes, 1889–1961
13. Site of Block E, razed 1988
14. City Center, Hennepin between Sixth and Seventh, 1982

Ca. 1940 　　　4 　　　　　　　　　　5 　　　6 　　　7

The 1995 view, looking north from near Seventh, shows that Hennepin has maintained a surprising degree of architectural integrity since the 1930s but has lost much of its vitality. Although Hennepin can still be a fairly lively place after dark, it lacks the snap and sparkle it once enjoyed, and only one regular movie theater (the Skyway) still operates on the avenue.

Part of the problem is that many of the small, and not always savory, businesses that once lined Hennepin have disappeared. In the 1980s, for example, the city of Minneapolis tore down the sleazy but animated Block E on the north side of Hennepin between Sixth and Seventh, leaving a gaping hole that as of 1995 had yet to be filled. Across the street, the construction of the oafish, introverted City Center complex in 1982 brought a big hunk of architectural deadweight to the avenue. An undulating

1927 8 9 10 11 12

canopy and new signs have since been attached to City Center in an effort to liven up the place, but even the gaudiest makeup cannot do much for a corpse.

The city has also made some unfortunate traffic decisions on Hennepin. The avenue is now one way, and that circumstance encourages fast vehicular traffic but does nothing for pedestrians. Hennepin is also devoid of on-street parking, which is one reason that it seems so barren.

But there have been positive trends as well. The restoration and reopening of the State and Orpheum Theaters (primarily for touring Broadway plays and concerts) gave a much-needed boost to Hennepin in the early 1990s. And by 1995 efforts were once again under way to find a suitable new development for Block E. As a result, it is possible that Hennepin will one day return to its traditional role as the place where Minneapolis goes to play.

Eighth Street South

East from Hennepin Avenue, 1946

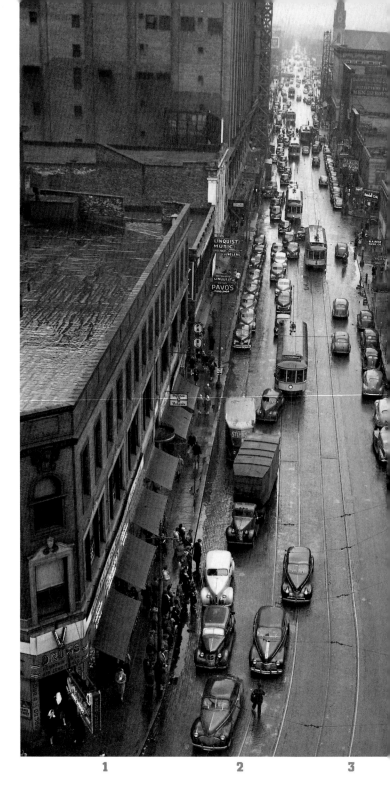

Two rainy-day views taken almost a half century apart highlight the mushrooming scale of downtown Minneapolis since the end of World War II. Both photographs were taken from the upper floors of the old Pence Building (now the Carmichael-Lynch Building) at the southwest corner of Eighth and Hennepin. Besides underscoring the volume of new construction along Eighth, the pictures reveal the dramatic growth of the downtown skyway system: five bridges now cross Eighth in the stretch between La Salle Avenue and Fourth Avenue South.

The 1946 view shows a street with humanly scaled brick and stone buildings of varied vintage. The newest building is the large addition to Dayton's Department Store under construction at Eighth and Nicollet. Undoubtedly the oldest structure is St. Olaf Catholic Church, built in 1874 as the Church of the Redeemer and substantially rebuilt after a fire in 1888. The church was to have its second and last trial by fire in 1953, when it burned down in a spectacular wintertime blaze. Among the numerous retail enterprises in view is Snyder's Drug Store, long a fixture at the corner of Eighth and Hennepin. Streetcars, automobiles, trucks, and pedestrians are also in plentiful supply, reflecting downtown's exceptional prosperity in the years immediately after the war.

The 1995 photograph reveals a very different street from that of fifty years ago. Eighth has been turned into a

1   2   3

one-way thoroughfare from which most parking is banned (a major reason why it seems so unfriendly to pedestrians, since parked cars act as a comforting buffer from traffic). Bordered by glassy modern skyscrapers, the street is also far more canyonlike than it used to be, and few of its prewar masonry structures remain.

Buildings and Places

1. Snyder's Drug Store building (now Shinders), Eighth and Hennepin, ca. 1910, ca. 1950
2. Dayton's Department Store addition, Nicollet between Seventh and Eighth, 1947 (Larson and McLaren)
3. St. Olaf Catholic Church, Eighth St. and Second Ave. S., 1874, 1888–1953
4. Walker Building, Eighth and Hennepin, ca. 1920
5. IDS Center, Seventh and Nicollet, 1973
6. La Salle Plaza, Eighth and La Salle, Ellerbe Becket, 1991

1   5 2   6

One survivor is the former Snyder's Drug Store building. Refaced and minus its top floor (probably lopped off to reduce tax assessments), the turn-of-the-century building is now home to a Shinders news and book store. Across the street, the La Salle Plaza development has also managed to preserve some of Eighth's old character by lim-

iting itself to a height of two stories near Hennepin. Meanwhile, Dayton's remains, as much of a Minneapolis institution as ever, although two skyways puncture its Eighth Street façade, while an adjoining parking ramp speaks to the needs of a downtown where the streetcars no longer run.

Tenth Street South

West from Marquette Avenue, 1931

These photographs depict something of a rarity in downtown Minneapolis: a view that has remained remarkably consistent over more than sixty years. Like most American cities, Minneapolis has tended toward block-sized downtown development projects in which old buildings and places are simply swept away. But alternate strategies of change are possible, and these scenes are a good example of how an incremental process can work over time, the new fitting in with the old rather than destroying it outright.

To be sure, change is visible here—most notably the disappearance of the old Minneapolis Public Library, which terminates the view down Tenth in the 1931 photograph. The library, a building that many Minneapolitans still fondly remember, was torn down in 1961 after the city's new library was completed at Fourth and Nicollet. The old building would have been a beautiful candidate for adaptive reuse, but that sort of thing did not happen much in the 1960s, and so the library was knocked down to make way for a parking lot.

Among the interesting details in the 1931 photograph is a horse-drawn milk wagon (right center), empty cans dangling behind it. Note also the billboard advertising a new car, probably a Chrysler, for a mere $895. Most of the buildings date from the early twentieth century and represent the second or third generation of structures in this neighborhood, which in the 1880s was largely residential.

1   6 2   4 5

The buildings have survived because this part of downtown—lying between the central core and the Convention Center and hotel district to the south—managed to escape heavy development pressure. It was a close call, however, since in the late 1980s a French development firm, LSGI, nearly won approval for a grandiose plan to create a huge domed shopping mall along Nicollet between Ninth and Eleventh. That mall would have wiped out much of what you see here.

The contemporary view shows one major new building—the University of St. Thomas at Tenth and La Salle—along with a delightful addition from the 1970s in the form of a musical mural (it is from a work by Ravel) on the side of the Schmitt Music Company building.

Buildings and Places

1. Handicraft Guild House (now shops and offices), Tenth and Marquette, William Channing Whitney, 1909
2. First Baptist Church, Tenth and Harmon, 1883 (Frederick B. Kees), 1887 (Long and Kees)
3. Minneapolis Public Library, Tenth and Hennepin, 1889–1961
4. Meyer (now Nicollet) Arcade, Tenth and Nicollet, 1909
5. Essex Building, Tenth and Nicollet, Ernest Kennedy, 1912
6. University of St. Thomas, Tenth and La Salle, Opus Architects and Engineers, 1992

Marquette Avenue

North from Ninth Street, 1952

Among the numerous financial institutions on Marquette, none offered a more striking skyline image than the Northwestern National Bank (now Norwest Bank) at Sixth and Marquette. The sixteen-story bank building, completed in 1929, was one of three major additions to the Minneapolis skyline that year. The other two are also visible here—the Rand Tower and the Foshay Tower (only part of its two-story base can be seen). But it was not the bank's large, if rather chunky, building that became a Minneapolis icon. It was, instead, the famous weatherball, an inspired piece of high-rise advertising in a part of the world where the weather is always on people's minds.

Mounted atop a 157-foot-high steel superstructure with huge lighted letters, the weatherball (which was a total of 367 feet above the street) made its debut in 1949. Its colorful code, drummed into the heads of Minnesotans by decades of incessant advertising, still lingers like a childhood prayer in thousands of memories—"White: cold in sight; red: warmer weather ahead; green: no change foreseen; blinking light by night or day: precipitation on the way." History does not record who coined this catchy jingle, but one can only hope that he or she was amply rewarded.

The big lighted ball gave out weather news until Thanksgiving Day 1982, when one of the largest fires in

Minneapolis history destroyed both the bank building and the vacant Donaldson's Department Store adjoining it. The ball and its superstructure were saved, however, and donated to the Minnesota State Fair in 1984. As of 1995, the weatherball remained in storage, a homeless piece of Minneapolis history.

Today the view down Marquette is dominated by Norwest Center, the art-deco-inspired skyscraper that rose from the ruins of the old bank building after it was demolished by explosives in 1984. Other new office towers have also sprouted up nearby, so that the avenue seems much more massively corporate than it did forty years ago. While some of these modern skyscrapers, especially Norwest Center and the IDS Center, are of high quality, it still would be awfully nice to have that winking, blinking weatherball back in action one day.

Buildings and Places

1. Doctors' Building (now Professional Building), Ninth and Marquette, 1917, ca. 1940s, 1980
2. Northwestern National Bank Building, Sixth and Marquette, Graham, Anderson, Probst, and White, 1929–84
3. Rand Tower, Sixth and Marquette, Holabird and Root, 1929
4. Foshay Tower (base only visible), Ninth and Marquette, 1929
5. Norwest Center, Sixth and Marquette, Cesar Pelli and Associates, 1989
6. AT & T Tower, Ninth and Marquette, Walsh Bishop Associates, 1991

Marquette Avenue

North from near Fifth Street, ca. 1906

It is comforting to think that in the old days downtown Minneapolis was a relatively stable place in which buildings were more than mere pawns in high-stakes development games. But it simply is not true. Take the case of the handsome neoclassic building at right. Constructed in 1906 as a new home for the First National Bank, it was a beautiful little banking temple. Prominent Minneapolis decorator John Bradstreet did the interiors, while the intricately detailed exterior included bronze doors and an ornate iron fence complete with lions' heads. Yet this building holds the dubious distinction of being perhaps the shortest-lived bank in Twin Cities history.

Buildings and Places

1. U.S. Courthouse and Post Office, Third and Marquette, office of the supervising architect of the U.S. Treasury, 1890–1961
2. Oneida Building, Fourth and Marquette, Long and Kees, 1888, 1890–ca. 1959
3. National Bank of Commerce, Fourth and Marquette, Harry Jones, 1889–1939
4. Northwestern National Bank, 409 Marquette Ave., Kees and Colburn, 1904–39
5. Boutell Brothers furniture store, Fifth and Marquette, ca. 1890 (Charles S. Sedgwick), 1905–ca. 69
6. First National Bank, Fifth and Marquette, Robert W. Gibson, 1906–14
7. U.S. Courthouse, Fourth and Marquette, 1960
8. One Hundred Fifth Street South, Fifth and Marquette, 1985, 1988
9. Soo Line Building, Fifth and Marquette, 1914

7   8   9

Less than eight years after its completion, it was torn down to make way for a much larger structure—the sixteen-story First National–Soo Line Building that still occupies the site. Another bank building in this photograph—the Northwestern National Bank just down Marquette near Fourth—did not fare much better. Built in 1904 and described by the *Minneapolis Journal* as "solid enough to last for ages," it was gone by 1939.

Given this tendency toward rapid replacement of buildings in downtown Minneapolis, it should come as no surprise that every structure visible in the 1906 photograph has vanished. The National Bank of Commerce, like its neighbor the Northwestern Bank, came down in 1939. The multitowered U.S. Courthouse and Post Office, some-

thing of an architectural lemon from the start, fell to the wrecker in 1961. The Boutell Brothers store, rebuilt after a 1905 fire and a favorite place for Minneapolitans to buy furniture since the 1870s, survived the longest, remaining in business until about 1969.

Today this part of Marquette consists largely of office buildings, with residential high-rises farther down the avenue in the old Gateway District. The Soo Line Building, which for the first fifteen years or so of its life was the tallest skyscraper in Minneapolis, is about the only old-timer left. Its skyline preeminence was eclipsed long ago by newer, taller office buildings, whose own lives—if what has happened along Marquette is any indication—may prove to be shorter than most people think.

Second Avenue and Fourth Street South

North across the Intersection, ca. 1896–98

The Northwestern Guaranty Loan (better known as the Metropolitan) Building—Minneapolis's most famous lost monument—dominates this turn-of-the-century photograph. With its awesome glass-and-iron light court and sculpted exterior walls of granite and sandstone, the Metropolitan was indeed something special, and its needless destruction continues to haunt the city over which it once towered so proudly.

Yet the Metropolitan was not the only building destroyed during Minneapolis's great frenzy of urban renewal in the 1950s and 1960s. The entire Gateway neighborhood around it also vanished, and this photograph makes clear just how great a loss that was.

Like other old sections of American downtowns, the Gateway was a place of magnificent detail, as cluttered and inviting as a Victorian parlor. The buildings visible here, including the Metropolitan, bristle with all manner of parapets, cornices, finials, chimneys, fire escapes, towers, domes, and other assorted protrusions (among them the peculiar open box—was it made to hold a sign?—on the building at far left).

Meanwhile the sidewalks are home to their own miscellany of objects—a mailbox, what appears to be a fire or

police alarm box (in front of the Gluek's sign), a wooden corner post (lower left) topped with an urn and decorated with cigar advertisements, fire hydrants, lampposts, and, in the foreground, a weirdly bent piece of pipe that resembles nothing so much as a large snake poised to strike some unsuspecting passerby. It is not a beautiful scene, but this little piece of Minneapolis looks wonderfully appealing, a place where a stroller would never lack entertainment for the eyes.

As for the dreary scene today, little needs to be said. The modern buildings are uniformly bland and soulless, as is the street itself. There is nothing to pull in the eye here, unless you are attracted to buildings that look like packing crates. The Towle Building, a suburban-style speculative office building that succeeded the Metropolitan, is especially uninspiring and qualifies as a prime example of what might be called reverse architectural progress.

Buildings and Places

1. Metropolitan Opera House (corner dome only visible), 320 Marquette Ave., Harry G. Carter, 1894–1937
2. Commercial building, Fourth St. and Second Ave. S., ca. 1880–ca. 1960
3. U.S. Courthouse and Post Office (top of one tower only visible), Third and Marquette, 1890–1961
4. Northern Hotel, Second Ave. S. between Third and Fourth, ca. 1880–ca. 1960
5. Northwestern Guaranty Loan (later Metropolitan) Building, Third St. and Second Ave. S., E. Townsend Mix, 1890–1961
6. U.S. Courthouse, Fourth and Marquette, Thorshov and Cerny, 1960
7. Towle Building, Second Ave. S. between Third and Fourth, Korsunsky, Krank, Erickson Architects, 1980
8. The Crossings Apartments, Washington and Second Ave. S., 1980

Second Avenue South

North from Tenth Street, 1929

The explosive growth of the Minneapolis skyline in the 1980s is strikingly evident in these two photographs. In 1929, this part of Second Avenue South was typical of what might be called the downtown fringe. Here, a few blocks away from the busy central core, was a modestly scaled environment with the usual mix of stores, apartments, and institutional buildings. Automobile-related businesses were especially attracted to the downtown edge at this time, and several are visible here.

The dominant object in this photograph is the Foshay Tower, still under construction, although its familiar thirtieth-floor signs (featuring ten-foot-high red letters) are already in place. The Foshay, an obelisk inspired by the Washington Monument, was the ultimate architectural folly of the 1920s in the Twin Cities. It was completed just as the stock market crashed, and its builder—a stock mar-

1   2   3   4   5

6　　　　　　　　　　　　　　3　7 8　　　　　　　　　9　　　　　10

ket plunger named Wilbur Foshay—was soon packed off to Leavenworth Prison for proving to be too creative a financier. No matter. The thirty-two-story tower was to rule the Minneapolis skyline for the next forty years and in the process become one of the city's most beloved buildings. For generations of schoolchildren, the tower's open-air observatory was the one and only place to catch a view of the city, and a field trip to the Foshay was always an eagerly awaited event.

Today, alas, the Foshay has become a runt among giants. The ferociously profitable (in the short term) real estate boom of the 1980s set off a frenzy of skyscraper construction in downtown Minneapolis, and the rather overwhelming results of that splurge are all too apparent here. So great have the changes been that only one building—the Minneapolis Athletic Club—is clearly visible in both photographs. Glass and steel behemoths of varying quality now lord over Second, while the small shops and stores have mostly disappeared. The result is an avenue that has plenty of architecture but not much life.

Buildings and Places

1. Foshay Tower, Ninth and Marquette, Magney and Tusler, 1929
2. Baker Building, Seventh St. and Second Ave. S., Larson and McLaren, 1926
3. Minneapolis Athletic Club, 615 Second Ave. S., Bertrand and Chamberlin, 1915
4. St. Olaf Catholic Church (originally Church of the Redeemer), Eighth St. and Second Ave. S., 1874, 1888–1953
5. Minneapolis City Hall, Fifth St. and Third Ave. S., built 1889–1906
6. Kinnard (originally International) Center, Second Ave. S. between Ninth and Tenth, Ellerbe Associates and Walsh Bishop Architects, 1984, 1986
7. First Bank Place, Sixth St. and Second Ave. S., Pei, Cobb, Freed, and Partners, 1992
8. St. Olaf Catholic Church, Eighth St. and Second Ave. S., Thorshov and Cerny, 1954
9. Hennepin County Government Center, Fifth St. at Third Ave. S., John Carl Warnecke Associates, 1973
10. Piper Jaffray Tower, Ninth St. and Third Ave. S., 1984

Third Avenue South

North from Twelfth Street, 1949

Two vanished hotels—the Leamington and the Curtis—dominate this view down Third Avenue South. Both were built around the turn of the century, at a time when the southern part of downtown was still largely residential. The hotels, in fact, replaced a pair of mansions belonging to one of Minneapolis's wealthiest families. The Fred C. Pillsbury house, built in 1888, once occupied the site of the Curtis, while the George A. Pillsbury mansion from the 1870s was cleared to make way for the Leamington.

The Curtis advertised itself as the "Largest Hotel in the Upper Midwest," with eight hundred rooms, many of which served a residential clientele. The building began life in 1903 as the Curtis Court apartments but was later expanded greatly with the construction of two twelve-story wings. Owned by three generations of the same family, the Curtis was never an expensive place. Even so, it attracted its share of notable visitors, among them Sir Tyrone Guthrie, who always stayed at the Curtis on his frequent visits to Minneapolis.

The seven-hundred-room Leamington, built in 1912 (with several later additions), was much more of a convention hotel than its competitor across the street. Both hotels, however, benefited enormously when the Minneapolis Auditorium opened a few blocks away in 1927. During its long life, the Leamington became well known for catering to the political crowd, especially after

its purchase by Minneapolis businessman (and DFL insider) Bob Short in 1964.

Dwight Eisenhower and Richard Nixon stayed at the Leamington, as did John F. Kennedy, Lyndon Johnson, Hubert H. Humphrey, Ronald Reagan, and a host of other prominent political figures. Perhaps the hotel's best-known architectural feature was its Hall of States, a three-thousand-seat meeting and banquet room completed in 1956 and the scene of many a political gala. Two other popular meeting rooms—the Hall of Presidents and the Hall of Cities—completed the hotel's convention facilities.

By the 1970s, both hotels were fading in the face of new competition, and the surprise is not that they disappeared but that they survived as long as they did. The Curtis was the first to close its doors and was dynamited into rubble in 1984. The Leamington came down six years later, to be replaced by a parking ramp and transit hub.

Today's view down Third still offers some familiar sights, including the Foshay Tower and the old Vocational High School. But without its longtime hotel residents, the street seems a bit forlorn, like someone trying to cope with the loss of two dear old friends.

Buildings and Places

1. Foshay Tower, Ninth and Marquette, 1929
2. Second Church of Christ Scientist, Eleventh St. and Second Ave. S., Edward S. Stebbins with William Channing Whitney, ca. 1898–ca. 1950
3. Leamington Hotel, Tenth St. and Third Ave. S., 1912 (F. E. Lockwood), 1955, 1961–90
4. Northwestern Bell Telephone (later US West) Building, Fifth St. and Third Ave. S., 1931
5. Curtis Hotel, Tenth St. and Third Ave. S., 1903, ca. 1911 (Lindstrom and Almars), ca. 1919 (Long and Lamoreaux)–84
6. Minneapolis Vocational High School (now Century Plaza), Twelfth St. and Third Ave. S., 1932 (Edward H. Enger), 1940, ca. 1980s
7. Second Church of Christ Scientist, Twelfth St. and Third Ave. S., 1952
8. Leamington Municipal Ramp and Transit Hub, Tenth St. and Third Ave. S., Ellerbe Becket, 1992
9. Piper Jaffray Tower, Ninth St. and Third Ave. S., Hammel, Green, and Abrahamson, 1984
10. IDS Data Center (site of Curtis Hotel), Tenth St. and Third Ave. S., Architectural Alliance, 1990

Portland Avenue and Grant Street

North toward Downtown, 1957

This pair of views shows, in a dramatic way, the phenomenal growth of the Minneapolis skyline since the 1950s. In the 1957 photograph, Wilbur Foshay's folly still towers over its environs with absolute authority. The Foshay's undisputed skyline hegemony was a function not only of its height but also of its location toward the southern end of downtown, where there were few other tall buildings. Only the large sign atop the Curtis Hotel offers even a hint of vertical competition. Farther away, the Rand Tower—completed about the same time as the Foshay—cuts a notable figure of its own, as does the Northwestern National Bank weatherball.

Prominently featured in the foreground is a Standard Oil service station (Jerry and Herb's) of the kind that first appeared in the 1940s and was heavily influenced by Walter Dorwin Teague's famous "box" prototype for Texaco stations in 1937. Thousands of these Standard stations—crisp and sophisticated examples of modernist design—once dotted roadsides across America.

Visible behind the Standard station is a large brick structure on Fifth Avenue South that was for many years home to the city's oldest synagogue, the Sh'are Tof Temple. By this time, however, the building was occupied

2   6   7   4   8   9   10

by the Jehovah's Witnesses and was nearing the end of its
life. Also visible to the right of the Standard station is the
upper floor (with arched windows) of the Oakland
Apartments, one of several nineteenth-century brick row
houses in this part of downtown.

Today's view is surprising, if only because the foreground has changed only moderately in almost forty years.
The Standard station, for example, has become a Unocal
outlet, but the building is pretty much the same, with new
signage and an extra service bay the only notable alterations. The background, however, has changed mightily,
with the poor Foshay resembling a child in a world of
steroidal adults. Still, there is no denying that the skyline
that erupted out of the building boom of the 1980s has
given downtown Minneapolis a muscular feel and a sense
of ambitious bigness it never had before.

Buildings and Places

1. Curtis Hotel, Tenth St. and Third Ave. S., 1903, ca. 1911, ca. 1919–84
2. Foshay Tower, Ninth and Marquette, 1929
3. Sh'are Tof Temple (later Kingdom Hall), 903 Fifth Ave. S., ca. 1904–ca. 69
4. Standard (now Unocal) service station, Portland and Grant, ca. 1950s
5. Adams (originally Oakland) Apartments, Tenth St. and Fifth Ave. S., Frederick A. Clark, 1888
6. IDS Center, Seventh and Nicollet, 1973
7. Piper Jaffray Tower, Ninth St. and Third Ave. S., 1984
8. Norwest Center, Sixth and Marquette, 1989
9. First Bank Place, Sixth St. and Second Ave. S., 1992
10. Metropolitan (originally Lincoln) Center, Eighth St. and Fourth Ave. S., Kohn Pedersen Fox, 1986

Grant Street

West from near Spruce Place, 1949

Few Minneapolis neighborhoods can match the urbanity of the Loring Park district. With its mixture of apartments, houses, shops, restaurants, churches, theaters, art museums, and parks, the Loring area offers a kind of urban experience that is disappearing from many American cities. Two historic photographs—both depicting parts of the block bounded by Spruce Place, La Salle Avenue, and Grant and West Fourteenth Streets—give a sense of how the neighborhood evolved over the years.

Originally the neighborhood was devoted almost exclusively to housing, as shown in an 1888 photograph looking east on Fourteenth toward La Salle and Nicollet. The wooden row house at left looks to be a quickly built speculative project, and its appearance in what was then an area of mostly single-family housing signals the development pressures to come. Row houses of this period were almost always rental properties, and that is undoubtedly the case here. The building's well-dressed residents, including several children, have come out on their front porches to pose for the picture, which may well have been taken on a Sunday.

A much later photograph shows another corner of the same block in 1949. By the time of this view, looking west toward Grant Street's termination at Loring Park, single-family homes had disappeared, replaced by large brick apartment buildings and institutional structures. Among the walk-up apartment blocks on the south side of Grant is the Brentwood, which also offered a corner grocery store in the basement. Such stores, once a gracious urban amenity to be found in most apartment-house districts, have become all but extinct in the age of the gas-and-go convenience store.

The north side of Grant in the 1949 view displays one of the Loring neighborhood's lost monuments—Central Park Terrace, a great turreted row house also known as "The Castle." It consisted originally of eighteen three-story townhouses, each with ten rooms, all elaborately decorated. Like most early row houses, Central Park Terrace never caught on with affluent renters, and it was soon subdivided into apartments.

Today's view down Grant is different, but not terribly so. The Brentwood (renamed and minus its corner grocery) still stands, while new apartments (built as part of the Loring Greenway project just to the north) have replaced Central Park Terrace. These new apartments are not of the quality of the old row house, but they fit in well enough. In this respect, they demonstrate how it is possible to change a piece of the city without destroying its fundamental character.

1888 **1**

2   3   4

2   5   3   6

Harmon Place

Northeast from Thirteenth Street, ca. 1930s

There are at least a few streets in downtown Minneapolis where change has not been synonymous with the wholesale destruction of old buildings. One such street is Harmon Place. As these photographs make clear, the street's backdrop—the downtown skyline—has assumed a completely new look over the past sixty years. Yet Harmon itself has maintained a refreshing degree of architectural stability, largely because it is too remote from the downtown core to attract the glittering eyes of large-scale developers.

In the 1930s, the lower part of Harmon was home to much of the city's automotive trade, with the steeple of First Baptist Church providing a godly counterpoint to the street's motorized devotion to mammon. Once, Harmon had been almost exclusively residential, but the flourishing automobile business drove out most housing—the Kenosha Apartments being an exception—after the turn of the century. Signs for Ford, Cadillac, and Nash (not to mention a billboard touting Gluek's Beer) are visible, and more dealers could be found farther down the street. Goodyear and Firestone tire dealers are also represented, as are a variety of other auto-related businesses. All are housed in handsome, straightforward brick buildings that create a pleasing presence on the street.

Today's view, which shifts the perspective a bit to bring in more of the modern skyline, shows that while a huge array of new buildings have bloomed in the background,

1   2   8 3 4   9   6   10   7

Harmon has much the same character as it did in the 1930s. To be sure, the auto businesses are mostly gone (though there is still a Firestone dealer at Twelfth), and a few old buildings have vanished. As a whole, however, Harmon remains remarkably intact.

This happened not only because big developers went elsewhere but also because the simple brick buildings along Harmon have proved to be so readily adaptable over the years. With large free-span interiors and solid construction, the old auto stores and dealerships can be used for just about any purpose, as a variety of small businesses have discovered. Not all of the alterations have been for the better—note, for example, what happened to the windows of the Sullivan Motor Company at far right. Nor does Harmon possess the splendid array of signs that gave it such a lively look in the 1930s. Even so, it remains one of the most approachable, humanly scaled streets left in downtown Minneapolis.

Buildings and Places

1. Automobile dealership (now W. A. Holden Co.), 1208 Harmon, ca. 1910
2. Kenosha Apartments (now condominiums), Twelfth and La Salle, ca. 1900
3. First Baptist Church, Tenth and Harmon, 1883, 1887
4. Minneapolis YMCA (now La Salle Apartments), Ninth and La Salle, 1919 (Long, Lamoreaux, and Long), 1994
5. Minnesota (later Radio City) Theater, Ninth and La Salle, Graven and Mayger, 1928–59
6. Cadillac dealership (later Bill Boyer Ford, now Hammel Green and Abrahamson, Inc.), Twelfth and Harmon, ca. 1910, 1980
7. Sullivan Motor Co. (now B.G.E.A. Building), Thirteenth and Harmon, ca. 1910
8. La Salle Plaza, Eighth and La Salle, 1991
9. University of St. Thomas, Tenth and La Salle, 1992
10. IDS Center, Seventh and Nicollet, Johnson and Burgee with Edward Baker and Associates, 1973

Loring Park

South from Harmon Place near Hennepin Avenue, ca. 1890

L oring Park began life in 1883 as Central Park, a name that did not accurately describe its place in the city. In truth, the park (renamed in 1890 in honor of early Park Board President Charles Loring) has always been a bit away from the center of things, occupying a transitional zone between downtown and the tony residential and cultural district around Lowry Hill. It is this mixed quality that makes the park and its

surroundings such an interesting part of Minneapolis. And it is precisely because the Loring Park area offers a little bit of everything that it remains one of the city's most inviting environments.

The historic photograph shows the park at a time when its surrounding streets were almost entirely residential. By the 1890s, in fact, a substantial mansion district had grown up around the park, especially to the north along Harmon Place and to the south on Fifteenth Street, Oak Grove Street, and Clifton and Groveland Avenues. Much of this development was spurred by improvements to the park that began almost immediately after its acquisition in 1883. The Minneapolis Park Board enlarged the pond by removing boggy areas, planted trees, built paths, and constructed an iron footbridge across the narrows of the lake. This work was done in accord with a plan prepared by

1

Horace Cleveland, the great landscape architect who did so much to shape park systems in the Twin Cities in the late 1800s.

The Loring Park area began to change in character after the turn of the century as commercial activity spread south from downtown along Harmon and Hennepin. One by one the old mansions fell, among them the magnificent Samuel C. Gale house at 1600 Harmon, torn down in 1933. The south side of the park gradually took on a new look as well, with institutional, religious, and apartment buildings rising in place of many of the old houses.

The 1995 view, shot from the roof of the Loring Bar and Cafe, shows the extent of this transformation. The mansions visible in the 1890 view are all gone, and apartment buildings form an almost solid wall along Fifteenth Street. The park itself, however, has retained its basic form

and character (although the lake appears to have shrunk a bit) and continues to play a vital role in the life of the neighborhood.

Buildings and Places

1. Dr. Jacob Tourtellate house, 505 Fifteenth St. W., ca. 1880–ca. 1920
2. Summit House condominiums, 400–410 Groveland Ave., ca. 1968
3. Loring Park Office Building (site of Tourtellate house), Fifteenth and Oak Grove, Hewitt and Brown, 1924
4. Hennepin Avenue United Methodist Church (steeple only visible), 511 Groveland Ave., 1916
5. Cathedral Church of St. Mark (tower only visible), Hennepin and Oak Grove, 1911

2   3 4   5

Hennepin and Lyndale Avenues (The Bottleneck)

South from Vineland Place, 1937

Among the traffic terrors that once existed in Minneapolis, none was more daunting than the infamous Bottleneck, where Hennepin (lower left to upper right) and Lyndale came together like scissor blades. Negotiating the Bottleneck in heavy traffic was an almost Parisian experience—the vehicles seemed to come at you from all manner of unexpected places and it was every driver for himself or herself. Yet this spectacularly acute intersection, created by Hennepin's angled disregard for the main Minneapolis grid, was also at the center of one of the city's finest collections of buildings and parks.

Bracketed by Loring Park on the east and the Parade Grounds on the west, the Bottleneck marked an elegant transition zone between downtown and the Lowry Hill mansion district. Churches, institutional buildings, and grand apartment houses grew up around it, posing in monumental splendor amid the greenery. It was, quite simply, the most urbane place in Minneapolis for half a century.

Among the buildings that contributed to this effect was the Plaza Hotel, from which the 1937 photograph was taken. Built in 1906, the six-story hotel had 125 rooms and a rooftop garden that must have offered splendid views of the city. The Hennepin Avenue side of the hotel can be seen in a 1946 photo looking north toward the domed Basilica of St. Mary. Note how buildings define the west side of Hennepin here, providing a crisp urban edge for Loring Park. Incidentally, it is not known why all the streetcars are backed up in this scene, but most likely there was a derailment or other mishap somewhere down the line.

The historic Bottleneck disappeared in the 1960s when Interstate 94 was tunneled beneath the flanks of Lowry Hill. The 1995 view, taken from the Irene Hixon Whitney Bridge by the Minneapolis Sculpture Garden, looks down into the maw of the tunnel at virtually the exact spot where the Plaza Hotel once stood. Vehicles and the vast infrastructure devoted to them dominate this scene, and what was once a classy (if, from the driver's point of view, challenging) intersection is now a great gash separating downtown from the residential neighborhood beyond.

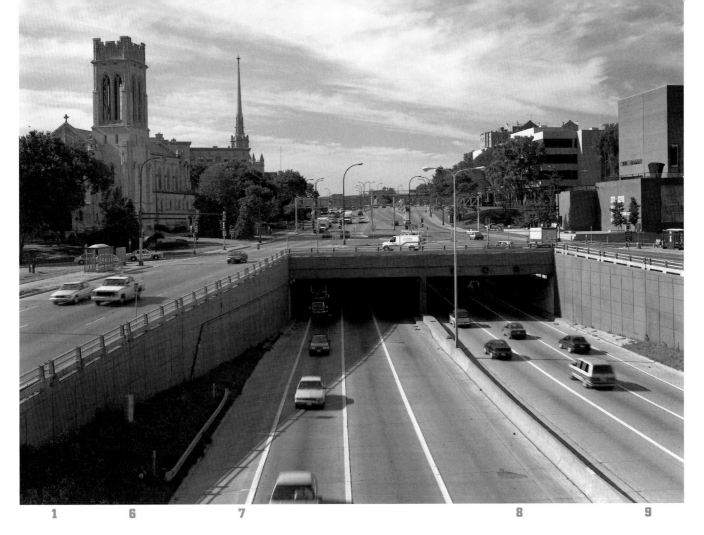

1   6   7   8   9

Buildings and Places

1. Loring Park

2. Thomas Lowry Memorial, Hennepin and Lyndale, Karl Bitter, 1915, 1967 (moved to Hennepin and Emerson)

3. Virginia Apartments, Hennepin and Lyndale, Harry Jones, 1900–ca. 64

4. Plaza Hotel, Hennepin and Kenwood Pkwy., Walter J. Keith, 1906–60

5. Basilica of St. Mary, Hennepin and Sixteenth St., Emmanuel L. Masqueray, 1914

6. Cathedral Church of St. Mark, Hennepin and Oak Grove, Hewitt and Brown, 1911

7. Hennepin Avenue United Methodist Church, 511 Groveland Ave., Hewitt and Brown, 1916

8. North American Life and Casualty Co. (now Allianz, Inc.), 1750 Hennepin Ave., Lang and Raugland, 1947

9. Walker Art Center, Vineland Pl. and Lyndale, Edward Larrabee Barnes, 1971

1946   4   5   1

Third Street South

West from Fourteenth Avenue South, ca. 1938

Historic street scenes often tend to show off cities at their best, depicting lively and beautiful places whose passing is just cause for regret. But picture postcard views of the past obscure the reality of what much of St. Paul and Minneapolis were really like in the good old days. This photograph from about 1938, looking along Third Street South toward downtown Minneapolis, serves as an antidote to such nostalgia.

The scene depicts a section of Third at the western edge of what is now known as the Cedar–Riverside neighborhood. It shows a hardscrabble piece of the city occupied by a well-worn mixture of sheds, houses, apartments, taverns, brick industrial buildings, and weedy vacant lots. Dirt streets add to the rough and ragged look of the place, although the crew at work on Third appears to be preparing for a paving project or some other public improvement.

At the time of this photograph, the Cedar–Riverside neighborhood—built up largely in the nineteenth century—was already considered one of the most blighted in the city. Like most neighborhoods around the fringes of downtown, it had developed before zoning laws, which explains its haphazard mingling of uses. The neighborhood was also home to an unusually large number of saloons and liquor stores, a circumstance that arose because Cedar–Riverside

1 2

lay just beyond the original city liquor patrol limits. At least two taverns are visible, including Eddie's Place (at far right), whose overhanging sign advertises Kato Beer.

Cedar–Riverside underwent extensive urban renewal in the 1960s and 1970s, much of it sparked by the University of Minnesota's decision to build a new West Bank campus. Along with all of the new buildings came a new freeway, Interstate 35W, which swallowed up even more of the old neighborhood. The 1995 view down Third was taken from a spot along the interstate's right-of-way. Cut off from downtown by the freeway's wide trench, Third now ends at a cul-de-sac just west of Fourteenth. Third resumes, however, on the other side of the interstate at Twelfth near the big beige bulge of the Hubert H. Humphrey Metrodome, a structure that the impoverished residents of Cedar–Riverside fifty years ago could hardly have imagined.

Buildings and Places

1. Minnesota Linseed Oil Paint Co. (now Valspar Corp.), Third St. and Eleventh Ave. S., Long and Long, 1904
2. Advance Thresher Building and Emerson-Newton Plow Co. (now Thresher Square), Third and Park, 1900 (Kees and Colburn), 1904, 1984
3. Hubert H. Humphrey Metrodome, Fifth and Chicago, Skidmore, Owings, and Merrill and others, 1982
4. Federal Building and Courthouse (under construction), Fourth St. and Fourth Ave. S., to be completed 1996

Minneapolis
Neighborhoods

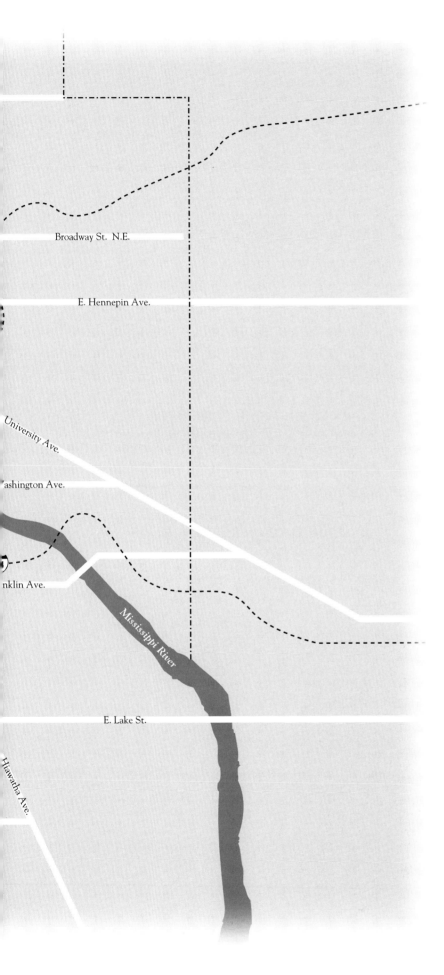

Broadway St. N.E.

E. Hennepin Ave.

University Ave.

ashington Ave.

nklin Ave.

Mississippi River

E. Lake St.

Hiawatha Ave.

Minneapolis
Neighborhoods

A. Central Avenue

B. West Broadway Avenue

C. Plymouth Avenue

D. Sixth Avenue North (Olson Memorial Highway)

E. Park Avenue

F. East Lake Calhoun Parkway

G. Hennepin Avenue, from Colfax Avenue

H. Hennepin Avenue, from Lake Street

I. Lake Street, from Lyndale

J. Lake Street and Hiawatha Avenue

K. Franklin Avenue

L. Cedar Avenue

M. Seven Corners

This street map was drawn from a 1938 map of Minneapolis.

Central Avenue

North from Twenty-third Avenue Northeast, 1956

The evolution of neighborhood shopping streets like Central Avenue tends to be more gradual than that of downtown commercial streets, just as small towns tend to change less quickly than big cities. In both cases, development pressure—usually far more intense in big places than in small ones—accounts for the difference.

Still there is no question that Central has evolved, as a 1923 view looking north from near Third Avenue Northeast reveals. At the time, this section of Central was as much residential as commercial, and most of the buildings were of wooden construction (one exception being the 165-foot-high gas storage tank in the distance). Like many streetcar strips, Central steadily became more commercial as businesses moved in to take advantage of the trade brought by trolleys, which began running along the avenue in 1891.

The 1956 photograph of Central looking toward Lowry Avenue shows a street devoted entirely to commerce—a

situation that had not changed by 1995. While a few buildings (such as the Arion Theater) have vanished over the past forty years, most survive, albeit in modified form. Note, however, that the mortuary at right appears to have undergone only modest changes since 1956, suggesting that there is a certain timelessness to the business of death.

Although the buildings in these two photographs have not changed dramatically, the avenue's overall appearance has. This is largely due to changes in the avenue's "street furniture"—all the stuff along streets besides the buildings themselves. The 1956 picture shows a street with a highly varied visual menu. Signs hang over the sidewalks; flagpoles, struts, and chimneys rise from rooftops; light poles sport ornamental globes; parked cars clutter the curbs; and even the roadway itself (which was being widened at the time) has a busy texture marked by brick pavers and streetcar tracks.

By contrast, the 1995 photograph shows simplified building fronts, modest signs, a lack of rooftop clutter, modern cobra-head lights, limited on-street parking, smooth asphalt over the old brick, and trees planted along the sidewalk. It is all very orderly and rather boring. Even so, Central has managed to retain much of its commercial vibrancy, no mean accomplishment at a time when many old streetcar strips—West Broadway on the North Side comes to mind—have fallen on hard times.

1923   1

Buildings and Places

1. Minneapolis Gas Light Co. storage tank, Broadway and Polk St., ca. 1910–ca. 60
2. Arion Theater, Central between Twenty-third and Twenty-fourth, 1910–ca. 57 (closed)
3. Dovre Hall, Central and Twenty-fourth, ca. 1900
4. O. E. Larson Mortuary (now O. E. Larson-Osborne Mortuary), Central and Twenty-third, ca. 1920, ca. 1950

West Broadway Avenue

West from near Fourth Street, 1949

To anyone who grew up on the North Side of Minneapolis in the years after World War II (as I did), West Broadway functioned as the big city equivalent of a small town Main Street. In fact, this photograph from November 1949 (yes, the holiday decorations went up awfully early even then) could be mistaken for a scene from some bustling small town were it not for the streetcar tracks running down the middle of Broadway.

The tracks explain why Broadway developed as it did.

A classic streetcar strip street, Broadway saw its first tracks (for horsecars) in 1882. By 1891 electric streetcars were in service all down the avenue, and the area quickly evolved into a shopping and entertainment hub for the mostly blue-collar community on the North Side.

There was nothing fancy about Broadway, even in its prime. The store buildings, some dating back to the late nineteenth century, were mostly of the two- or three-story brick variety, although by 1949 many had already received modern façades. Even so, the street was in its own way a complete world. You could buy almost anything on Broadway—clothes for the family at one of several department stores, toys and notions at Woolworth's, even a new car from Northside Chevrolet (its signs can be seen in front of the church tower on the left side of the street).

There were also restaurants, taverns and liquor stores, grocery stores, banks, barber shops, hardware stores, and

no fewer than three movie theaters (the Empress, the Broadway, and the Paradise). The modest marquee of the Empress, which like its two theatrical companions on Broadway is long since gone, can be seen here (though only faintly) in front of the tall Clover Leaf sign on the right.

The West Broadway neighborhood has become increasingly impoverished in recent years, and much of the street has taken on a mean, bedraggled look. Most of the old stores are gone, replaced (if at all) by cut-rate retailers or modern strip malls, like the one at left. A Target store has also made its appearance behind the usual big parking lot. Meanwhile, on-street parking—so vital to both the appearance and function of any good urban thoroughfare—has been all but banned, with the result that Broadway is now a street for cars rather than people. Remarkably, however, one business—Friedman's

Department Store—has managed to survive all the changes and remains in the old Gatzemeier Block at Fourth and Broadway, where it has been since 1930.

Buildings and Places

1. Broadway Covenant Church (originally Swedish Evangelical Mission Church), Aldrich at Broadway, ca. 1900–ca. 57
2. Clover Leaf Creamery (now Kemp's Dairy Products), 420 W. Broadway, 1912
3. Empress Theater, 412 W. Broadway, 1908–ca. 77
4. Gatzemeier Block (Friedman's Department Store), 400 W. Broadway, 1894
5. Broadway Center shopping mall, Fourth and Broadway, ca. 1980s

Plymouth Avenue

West toward Morgan Avenue, ca. 1945

Of all the old neighborhood commercial streets in Minneapolis, few have experienced more overwhelming change during the modern era than Plymouth Avenue on the North Side. Once home to scores of small shops, many owned by Jewish merchants, the avenue today runs through a predominantly black community and has lost much of its commercial vitality. This transformation is especially noticeable in the area around Morgan Avenue, which for many years was the heart of Plymouth's shopping district.

Jews first began moving into Minneapolis in significant numbers around 1890 as part of a great wave of immigration from Europe to America. By 1907, an estimated forty-five hundred Jews were living on the city's North Side, a number that increased to more than eleven thousand by the mid-1930s. There was also a sizable Jewish community on the South Side, although a 1936 survey indicated that about 70 percent of the city's Jews were North Side residents. At first, Sixth Avenue North (now Olson Memorial Highway) was the favored locale for many Jewish merchants. But as the Jewish population gradually spread northward, Plymouth also became a major shopping area for the community.

The historic view gives a good sense of the ambiance of the Plymouth Avenue commercial district during the 1940s. The buildings in view are simple brick affairs, one story high, and mostly built between about 1910 and 1925. Yet these two blocks appear to harbor just about every kind of business needed to make a neighborhood a good place. Businesses in view include a bakery, a fresh fish store, a printing company, a drugstore, a delicatessen (Abe's), a grocery, an auto garage, and even a small movie theater (the Homewood).

Today all remnants of the old commercial strip at Plymouth and Morgan are gone, although a few stores catering to the area's substantial black population remain. A race riot on July 17, 1965, that brought out the National Guard caused significant damage along Plymouth, and many merchants subsequently left. A modern housing complex, a Minneapolis police substation, and large parking lots now occupy the south side of the avenue to either side of Morgan, leaving a sense of vacancy where once a lively world of commerce flourished.

Buildings and Places

1. Strimling Drugs, Plymouth and Morgan, 1933–ca. 59 (closed)
2. Abe's Delicatessen, Plymouth and Morgan, ca. 1945–ca. 54 (closed)
3. Homewood Theater, Plymouth and Newton, ca. 1920–ca. 52 (closed)

Sixth Avenue North (Olson Memorial Highway)

West from near Lyndale Avenue, 1922

Urban environments can change in many ways. Sometimes the alterations are quite subtle, the result of hundreds of small accretions and subtractions as human needs accommodate themselves to new circumstances. In other cases, however, a metamorphosis takes place, usually as a result of large-scale renewal or highway construction. Sixth Avenue North, now known along most of its route as Olson Memorial Highway, provides an especially striking example of such a transformation.

The 1922 photograph of Sixth, taken about a block east of Lyndale (which is the first cross street visible), shows a typical streetcar strip street. Small businesses and services—restaurants, billiard halls, drugstores, a laundry, a tailor's shop, doctors' offices—line the street, mixed with a few old dwellings that were probably apartments or rooming houses. This part of Minneapolis, near the once genteel Oak Lake subdivision, was not what would today be called an "upscale" neighborhood. Its population—which

by 1922 included many Jews and a small but growing number of blacks—was generally poor, and much of the housing stock was extremely dilapidated.

Considered a slum, the area was targeted for some of the earliest urban renewal projects in Minneapolis. In 1933 the Oak Lake neighborhood was cleared to become a new site for the city market. Five years later, a thirty-acre tract of deteriorated housing just south of Sixth near Bryant Avenue was leveled to make way for Sumner Field, the city's first public housing project. At about this same time came the biggest change of all, for in the mid-1930s buildings along the north side of Sixth were demolished to widen the street, which was later renamed Olson Memorial Highway (after former Minnesota Governor Floyd B. Olson). Other large renewal projects followed in the 1950s and 1960s.

Today Olson Highway is a six-lane traffic corridor leading into and out of downtown, and nothing whatsoever remains of the old Sixth Avenue or its brick and wooden storefronts. Lyndale Avenue has also taken on a new life in this area and now functions as a one-way frontage road for Interstate 94. Overall, the transformation depicted here has been so complete that it is hard to believe both photographs were taken from the same place.

Park Avenue

North from near Nineteenth Street East, 1905

Park Avenue was once the Summit Avenue of Minneapolis, a street of sumptuous mansions occupied by the city's business and professional elite. Most of the avenue's grand houses, designed by leading Minneapolis architects, were built in the 1880s between about Eighteenth and Twenty-eighth Streets. By 1887 the quality of the neighborhood was such that the *Saturday Evening Spectator,* a local newspaper, pronounced

Park Avenue "the finest residence section of Minneapolis." This circumstance was attributed not only to the avenue's convenient location just south of downtown but also to "the intelligent cooperation of an unusually enterprising class of citizens."

This cooperation took the form of a homeowners' group known as the Park Avenue Improvement Association. Founded in the mid-1880s, the association provided money to plant trees, to install sidewalks and curbs, and to ensure that Park Avenue in 1889 became the first Minneapolis street to receive asphalt paving. The association's wealthy members even went so far as to buy a house thought to be too close to the street so it could be moved back to align with the general setback along the avenue.

The 1905 view shows how the avenue looked during

1

1   2

its better days, although the most lavish houses on Park were actually south of Franklin Avenue. The scene here is a kind of upper-middle-class idyll of the period: big houses sporting front porches and gingerbread trim, carriages rolling down the tree-lined avenue, well-dressed children playing amid the genteel greenery of immaculately tended lawns.

But if there is one lesson to be learned about American cities, it is this: making a place is one thing, making it last another. By the early decades of this century, apartment buildings began to replace many of the mansions along Park, and the avenue's wealthier citizens gradually moved away. Later, the city widened Park and turned it into a one-way conduit into downtown, two "improvements" that

did not benefit its appearance. Today this part of Park runs through an area—the Phillips neighborhood—that is home to some of the city's poorest residents, and only a few fading remnants of the past (like the apartment building at left) serve as reminders of the very different world that once existed here.

Buildings and Places

1. Colonial Apartments, Nineteenth and Park, Harry Jones, 1894
2. First Bank Place, Sixth St. and Second Ave. S., 1992

East Lake Calhoun Parkway

Northwest from Thirty-sixth Street, ca. 1905

he chain of lakes in southwest Minneapolis is among the city's defining attributes, a source of civic pride and pleasure for more than a century. A gift of nature, the lakes are also—like other parts of the city—a product of human enterprise and ingenuity and as such are well removed from their natural state. Lake Calhoun, the largest of the lakes, is typical in this regard, since it attained its present form only after extensive dredging and filling.

The lake's history has some intriguing features, beginning with its name. Once known as Loon Lake, it was later rechristened in honor of John C. Calhoun, an odd honor for a Southerner who championed states' rights and slavery. In 1834 the lake became the site of the first white settlement in what is now Minneapolis. In that year, Samuel and Gideon Pond built a log cabin on the lake's east shore near Thirty-fifth Street, just a block or so north from where these photographs were taken. The brothers, from

Connecticut, were missionaries and worked, with limited success, to convert the local Dakota to Christianity.

The 1905 view shows the lake at a time when the Minneapolis Park Board was still in the process of acquiring shoreline, a task completed in 1909. Also yet to come was large-scale dredging of the lake designed to eliminate swampy areas that flooded in spring and made access difficult. The first big dredging project occurred between 1911 and 1915, and additional work was done from 1923 to 1925.

The lake as seen here was larger than it is today—the dredging and filling reduced Calhoun's size from 460 to about 425 acres. Note also that the parkway around the lake was not yet paved (that happened beginning in 1911

and was completed in the 1920s). However, numerous improvements were already in place by 1905, including many trees planted at water's edge and the horse-watering trough in the middle of the road. Another significant improvement came in about 1909 when ice-harvesting shacks on the north side of the lake (barely visible here) were removed.

The contemporary view reveals a number of changes to the shoreline since 1905. The low ornamental trees are gone, and bicycle and walking paths have replaced the old dirt road at water's edge. But the essentials have survived, and Lake Calhoun remains just what it was in 1905—a place for people to enjoy one of the great natural amenities in all of urban America.

Hennepin Avenue

South from Colfax Avenue, ca. 1895
South across Lake Street, ca. 1935

This pair of then-and-now views highlights the growth of one of Minneapolis's most successful and vibrant neighborhoods—the Uptown area centered at Hennepin and Lake. The older of the two pictures, taken just before the turn of the century, shows how the neighborhood began life as an almost exclusively residential district. Hennepin Avenue, cutting a diagonal through the South Minneapolis grid, served as the district's main thoroughfare. Initially the city's park board maintained this part of Hennepin as a boulevard, along which commercial development was prohibited. The view shows a Harriet streetcar (possibly a rebuilt horsecar at this early date) running down the avenue's wide median. All around are new single-family houses, their recent vintage indicated by, among other things, the modest size of trees along the boulevards. This was, in short, turn-of-the-century suburbia.

The neighborhood, and especially Hennepin Avenue, underwent a major transformation after 1900. What today

1

2

would be called the "buying power" of the area's generally well-to-do residents inevitably attracted commercial development. The park board gave up its no-commerce policy on Hennepin in 1905, and small businesses (along with numerous professional offices) soon began locating along the avenue. Modern brick apartment buildings appeared as well, and by the 1920s Hennepin was a much different street from the one it had been just thirty years before.

Today's view from Hennepin and Colfax reveals how complete the transformation was. Private homes are all but gone from the avenue, which now offers a somewhat chaotic but on the whole quite inviting mix of stores, offices, restaurants, and apartment buildings.

3   4   5   *Ca. 1935*

The second set of views, at Hennepin and Lake, shows the neighborhood's commercial crossroads and also offers an urban object lesson, which is that it is not always necessary to demolish buildings to make an old place work well in new times. In fact, it is the stability of the architectural ensemble at this intersection that has helped make it one of the most successful commercial sites in Minneapolis.

The view from 1935 reveals the intersection's formula for success: small, friendly brick buildings, handsomely adorned with stone or terra-cotta trim; lots of plate-glass windows; enough signs to keep things lively without causing eye strain; and a wide variety of shops and services. Note, for example, the large number of second-story signs for dentists, a handy thing for those who overindulged on sweets at Abdallah's Cafe, famous for its ice cream and chocolate confections. The one exotic building in this scene is the Granada Theater, a Moorish-styled "atmospheric" movie house complete with twinkling stars on the ceiling.

By 1995 the intersection had acquired a mostly new,

and mostly upscale, set of shops, restaurants, and services while retaining the bulk of its old buildings. In the early 1980s, the opening of the Calhoun Square shopping mall (created by hollowing out the turn-of-the-century brick building at the intersection's southeast corner) set the tone for much subsequent development in the area. Updated façades, a parking ramp, and some new and generally sympathetic buildings (such as a Gap store on the southwest corner) have also been added to the intersection's architectural amalgam. And while a few unfortunate changes have been made (most notably the decision to turn Lake into a one-way street), the intersection has lost none of its vitality or visual interest, and it remains one of the best places in Minneapolis to enjoy city life as it was meant to be.

Buildings and Places

1. Joseph O. Therien house, Hennepin and Colfax, 1893–1913
2. Apartment building (site of Therien house), Hennepin and Colfax, ca. 1915
3. Geanakoplos Building (now Calhoun Square), Hennepin and Lake, 1917 (A. L. Dorr), 1983
4. Granada (now Suburban World) Theater, Hennepin near Lake, Liebenberg and Kaplan, 1928
5. Commercial building (Liggett's Drug Store), Hennepin and Lake, ca. 1915–ca. 90s
6. Gap Clothing Store, Hennepin and Lake, 1993

3   4   6

Lake Street

East from Lyndale Avenue, 1906

The intersection of Lake Street and Lyndale Avenue was one of the earliest commercial nodes to develop near the Minneapolis lake district. One writer, in fact, has called this area "the Southdale of the 1880s and 1890s." That may be overstating the case, but there is no question that the intersection, often referred to as Lyndale Corners, was the largest shopping district in South Minneapolis by 1900. A number of factors—good access to public transportation, the prohibition of commercial development along nearby Hennepin Avenue until 1905, and the opening in 1896 of Nicollet Baseball Park a few blocks to the east—all contributed to the intersection's growth. When this photograph was taken, double streetcar lines down Lake had just been completed, further enhancing the commercial appeal of Lyndale Corners.

Perhaps the most intriguing buildings in this view are the three-story wooden commercial blocks at the southeast and northwest corners of the intersection. Quite similar in style, both buildings harken back to an earlier time, when wooden commercial structures were common, even in downtown Minneapolis. Fire codes gradually outlawed wood-frame construction for most commercial purposes, and by 1906 these two Victorian dowagers must have seemed rather quaint, especially with their small decorative balconies suspended over the street.

An impressive variety of businesses occupy the inter-

1   3   2

section, including a hardware store, a grocery, a meat market, a plumbing company, and a drugstore (denoted by the large mortar and pestle mounted on a post on the sidewalk at the southwest corner). The streets are hardly choked with traffic, but a couple of streetcars, several carriages, and that all-important bearer of liquid refreshment—a Pabst's beer wagon (at right)—provide a modicum of movement. It is also apparent that street work of some kind is under way along Lake, where piles of dirt and rubble can be seen next to the sidewalks. Neither Lake nor Lyndale was paved at this early date (Lake did not receive its first paving, in the form of wooden blocks, until 1913), and the intersection must have presented a challenging morass after a good rainfall.

The 1995 view shows that Lake and Lyndale remains a lively enough place, even if it has been overshadowed in recent years by the surge in upscale development at Hennepin, eight blocks to the west. As might be expected, all of the wooden buildings that once overlooked the intersection are gone. But several other structures from the 1906 view survive, including the distinctive stone-clad Crowell Block at the intersection's northeast corner.

Buildings and Places

1. Crowell Block, Lyndale and Lake, Joralemon and Ferrin, 1888
2. Paus Block (now Lyndale Building), Lyndale and Lake, Goodman and Fisk, 1887
3. Lyn-Lake Building, Lyndale and Lake, ca. 1930

Lake Street and Hiawatha Avenue

Northeast across the Intersection, 1954

Two types of businesses that have all but vanished from the Twin Cities—farm implement manufacturing and the mom-and-pop roadside drive-in restaurant—are represented in this photograph from 1954. The picture also gives a partial view of Tankar Super Gas, an independent service station of the kind that has become quite rare.

The structure that dominates this view, however, is the huge Lake Street plant operated by the Minneapolis-Moline Company, once the fifth largest maker of agricultural equipment in the United States. Built for the Minneapolis Steel and Machinery Company, the plant acquired its familiar name in 1929 when a merger of three companies produced Minneapolis-Moline. The company—which had another factory and its main office in Hopkins—employed 1,250 workers at the Lake Street plant as late as 1968, producing tractors like those seen parked next to the plant.

All those workers, of course, got hungry, and Jack's was close at hand to provide French fries, hamburgers, chicken, pork loins, and other fast-food delicacies. This was still the free-for-all era of roadside dining, and casually decorated joints like Jack's—note the chicken proudly affixed to the middle of each sign—were common sights. But franchises were also around, and at the far right of this view is a White Castle outlet that no doubt gave Jack a run for his money. A 1956 photograph of the intersection, looking south on Hiawatha across Lake, gives a better view of the White Castle in all of its porcelain-paneled glory.

The story of this intersection in the years that followed is, in many respects, the story of America. Production at Minneapolis-Moline began declining in the 1960s, and the Lake Street plant was closed in 1972 by a successor company, White Farm Equipment Company. Meanwhile, Jack's and hundreds of similar eateries also vanished as giant franchised fast-food operations like McDonald's and Burger King came to dominate the business. Today the site of the old Minneapolis-Moline factory is a Target store, while a vacant lot marks the site where Jack dished out all those pork loins.

1956

Franklin Avenue

East from Cedar Avenue, 1913

It is hard not to love this historic photograph, which is remarkable not only for its clarity but for its almost tactile sense of what urban life was really like in the old days.

To begin with, there were a lot of dirt streets. In St. Paul, for example, only about 14 percent of the streets had been paved as of 1916, and probably the figure in Minneapolis was not much better. Wet weather, of course, turned the dirt to mud. And with horse-drawn transportation still very common at this time, the mud was often laced with manure, forming what must have been a fragrant kind of street soup. Nonetheless, the fellow negotiating Franklin here in his Ford Model T seems ready for anything. He is wearing heavy gloves, an AAA shield adorns his radiator, and his face is a study in stalwart determination.

This picture also shows how rare mature trees were in some parts of the Twin Cities around the turn of the century. In fact, hardly a tree is in sight, which contributes greatly to the scene's bleak atmosphere. The lack of trees here (in part a consequence of the fact that this part of Franklin had no boulevards in 1913) contrasts sharply with the leafy look that pervades most of the Twin Cities today following decades of dedicated reforestation.

Another interesting feature of the photograph is that it demonstrates how casually different types of buildings were mixed together in the days before zoning laws took effect. Here, houses and storefronts seem to alternate amid a pro-

liferation of painted signs and billboards. In the early 1920s, both St. Paul and Minneapolis adopted zoning ordinances designed to segregate uses and promote efficient planning, with the result that many city streets have gradually lost some of their old variety.

Today the dreary street scene depicted in the 1913 picture has vanished, although the transportation wasteland that replaced it can hardly be described as an improvement. The original intersection of Franklin and Cedar is also gone, and the streets now meet more than a block east of their 1913 location. A Soo Line railroad bridge spans the site of the old intersection, where trains once crossed at grade. A photograph from about 1920 shows how the intersection appeared just before the bridge was built. The 1995 view reveals little except the barren fruits of progress along Franklin in the form of traffic, the inevitable road construction, and several high-rise apartments in the distance.

Ca. 1920

Cedar Avenue

North from near Fifth Street South, ca. 1890

Much of Cedar–Riverside was redeveloped in the 1960s and 1970s, but there are still a few places where the neighborhood maintains something of its historic character. One such place is along Cedar near Fifth, an intersection dominated for more than a century by the towered presence of Dania Hall.

A photograph from around 1890 shows this part of Cedar during the early years of the streetcar era. Note that trolley wires are strung on poles down the middle of Cedar, a fairly common arrangement that vanished with the arrival of automobiles. Delivery wagons provide about the only traffic competition for streetcars, since this was not a neighborhood where carriages would have been common. The small buildings along Cedar—mostly brick but a few still of the old wood-frame variety—reflect the neighborhood's lack of pretension.

The one building that stands out by virtue of its size and height is Dania Hall, which had opened just a few years before this photograph was taken. Built by a benevolent organization that assisted immigrant Danes, the hall included ground-floor shops, offices, a billiard parlor, club rooms, and an eight-hundred-seat auditorium on the upper floors. The hall was used by many of the neighborhood's ethnic groups over the years, although it was especially popular with Scandinavians.

Scandinavian-language vaudeville was born at Dania Hall, and a number of its alumni went on to careers as

1

2   1

national recording artists. The hall also attracted some notable speakers. Among them was Nobel-prize-winning Norwegian writer Knut Hamsun, who lived in Minneapolis for a time. In 1888 he delivered a series of lectures at Dania, the last of which—"Thoughts on Esthetics, Culture in Minneapolis"—was sufficiently critical to offend some of the city's cultural mavens.

A contemporary view reveals that quite a few of the buildings visible in 1890 are still around, including Dania Hall (which survived a 1991 fire but as of 1995 was vacant, shorn of its tower roof, and very much in need of an angel with deep pockets). Elsewhere, however, the neighborhood has changed enormously since 1890. The huge Cedar Square West project looms just to the west while to

the north stands the University of Minnesota's West Bank campus. Despite such developments, this stretch of Cedar continues to perk along with its collection of shops, taverns, and restaurants, which provide a welcome measure of funkiness in an otherwise institutional landscape.

Buildings and Places

1. Dania Hall, Cedar and Fifth St. S., Carl F. Struck, 1886
2. Holiday Inn (originally Radisson) Metrodome, 1500 Washington Ave. S., ca. 1985

Seven Corners

East along Washington Avenue toward Cedar Avenue, 1952

L ike its counterpart in St. Paul, the Minneapolis version of Seven Corners was created by the collision of two grid systems at the edge of downtown. In its original configuration, Seven Corners—which was nearly a block long and could actually be interpreted as two separate but adjacent intersections—marked the convergence of Washington and Cedar Avenues, Fifteenth Avenue South, and Second Street South. It must have been a befuddling place for neophyte drivers, and it is hard even today to become oriented in this part of town.

The 1952 photograph shows the southern end of the intersection, with Washington coming in from the lower left and curving due east toward its Mississippi River crossing a few blocks away. Another part of Washington splays to the right to connect to Cedar (where the semitrailer truck is waiting for a stoplight), while Fifteenth crosses from the far right to the upper left on its way north toward the Tenth Avenue Bridge.

Seven Corners at this time was considered a rather disreputable part of town—home to taverns, liquor stores, diners, low-rent apartments, and cut-rate retailers such as the Hagen Company, whose sign characterizes its proprietors as the "wildest traders" around. Large billboards were

1   2   3

also part of the intersection's grungy charm. The biggest billboard, for Old Thompson "Triple A Blend" whiskey, proclaims rather mysteriously that this fine example of the distiller's art was "wed in the wood."

Today Seven Corners has been reduced to a mere quartet of streets. Cedar and Fifteenth no longer continue north of the intersection, while the approach to the Washington Avenue Bridge is a block south of where it was in 1952. The southern approach to the Tenth Avenue Bridge has also been relocated to Nineteenth Avenue South. Many of these changes were made to accommodate increased traffic brought about by the opening of the University of Minnesota's West Bank campus in 1962.

Although the map of Seven Corners has changed drastically, its urban character has not, even with the addition of a high-rise Holiday Inn and other modern improve-

ments. The 1995 view, taken from a point near the 1952 photograph, shows that enough of the intersection's old brick buildings remain to provide a sense of historic continuity. A variety of small businesses, taverns, and entertainment venues continue to occupy these serviceable structures—proof that old places need not be destroyed.

Buildings and Places

1. Minneapolis Gas Light Co. storage tank, First St. and Twentieth Ave. S., ca. 1900–ca. 60
2. Apartment building (now Grandma's Saloon and Deli), 1810 Washington Ave. S., ca. 1890, ca. 1983
3. Simonson Block, Washington and Cedar, ca. 1890s
4. Holiday Inn Metrodome, 1500 Washington Ave. S., ca. 1985

St. Paul

Downtown

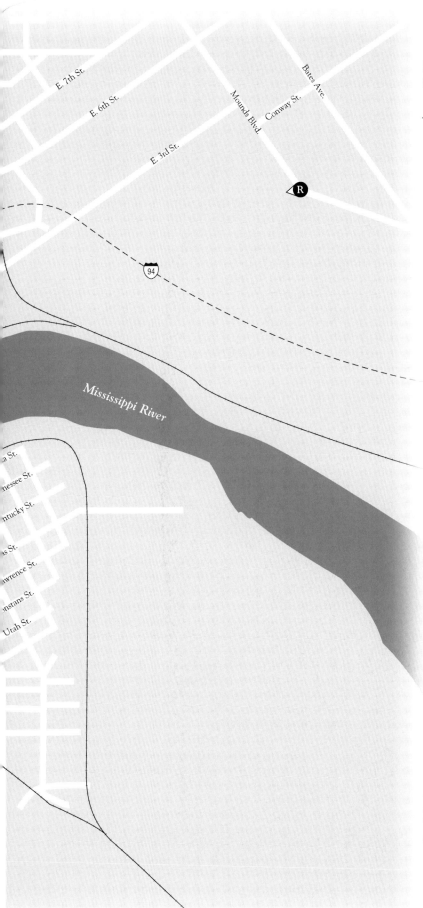

St. Paul
Downtown

A. Downtown Riverfront, from Harriet Island

B. Wabasha Street, from Sixth Street

C. Seventh Street

D. Sixth Street

E. Cedar Street, from Fourth Street

F. St. Peter, Washington, and Market Streets

G. Fifth Street, from Auditorium Street

H. Robert Street, from Fourth Street

I. Robert Street, from Sixth Street

J. Third Street, from Robert Street

K. Third Street, from Jackson Street

L. Fourth Street

M. Seventh Street, from near Sibley Street

N. Seventh Street, from Rosabel (Wall) Street

O. Great Northern Freight Terminal

P. Mississippi Street

Q. Rail Yards

R. Downtown and Riverfront, from Dayton's Bluff

S. Downtown, from Merriam's Hill

T. Wabasha Street, from Thirteenth Street

U. Cedar Street, from State Capitol

V. Twelfth Street

W. Fifth Street, toward Third (Kellogg) Street

X. Seven Corners

Y. Main Street

Z. Pleasant Avenue

AA. Downtown and Capitol Hill

BB. Downtown, from Sixth Street and Summit Avenue

CC. Downtown, from Smith Avenue High Bridge

This street map was drawn from a 1934 map of St. Paul.

Downtown Riverfront

North from Harriet Island, 1921

Downtown St. Paul has never managed to exploit the marvelous opportunity provided by its clifftop setting above the Mississippi River. For many years, as this photograph shows, the riverfront was a hodgepodge of warehouses, industrial buildings, and railroad tracks that formed an almost impenetrable barrier between the river and the downtown core just a few blocks away. This walling off of the river was not a deliberate act; it simply reflected the early, haphazard development of the city.

The railroads, for instance, took to the river purely as a matter of convenience, since the Mississippi Valley provided the best natural grade through the city. Creating this pathway for commerce required extensive work along the river, and over the years the railroads shaved away bluffs, filled in low areas, and constructed trestles, including the long wooden structure visible here. Despite its rather industrial flavor, the river nonetheless found its share of recreational users in the downtown area. The sleek wooden motorboats on display belong to members of the St. Paul Boat Club, organized in 1912 and based for many years on Harriet Island.

Although this scene looks quite appealing, there was in fact big trouble on the Mississippi at this time. Long an open sewer, the river had become so polluted by the early 1920s that the popular city beach on Harriet Island was closed, and even boaters were warned to avoid contact with the bacteria-laden waters.

A photograph from the same spot today shows that downtown remains largely walled off from the Mississippi, although fine waterfront views have been awarded to one group of captive citizens—inmates of the Ramsey County jail built in 1980. The old industrial buildings and warehouses visible in 1921 have either been torn down or converted to new uses, while the construction of Shepard Road along the river's edge in the early 1960s added yet another barricade to public use of the downtown waterfront.

Today, however, there are encouraging signs that the city may at last be ready to reclaim its riverfront. The Science Museum of Minnesota, for example, announced plans in 1995 to build a huge new complex near the Upper Landing (at far left) by the year 2000. The hope is that this project will spawn additional development and make the Mississippi waterfront what it always should have been: a vital and attractive part of downtown St. Paul.

Buildings and Places

1. St. Paul Public Library and Hill Reference Library, Fourth between Market and Washington, Electus Litchfield, 1917
2. Northern States Power Co. plant (now District Energy St. Paul, Inc.), Kellogg at Market, 1906
3. Federal Courts Building (now Landmark Center), Fifth between Market and Washington, 1892, 1902
4. West Publishing Co. (now Ramsey County Government Center West), Kellogg at St. Peter, ca. 1885, ca. 1900, ca. 1960s
5. St. Paul City Hall–Ramsey County Courthouse (tower only visible), Fourth and Cedar, Edward P. Bassford, 1889–1933
6. US West buildings, Fourth between Market and St. Peter, 1937 (Clarence Johnston, Jr.), 1968 (Ellerbe Associates), 1976
7. St. Paul City Hall–Ramsey County Courthouse, Kellogg and Wabasha, 1931 (Holabird and Root with Ellerbe Architects), 1993 (Wold Architects)
8. Ramsey County Adult Detention Center, Kellogg and Wabasha, Wold Assn., 1980

Wabasha Street

North from near Sixth Street, ca. 1922

The first Mississippi River bridge in St. Paul was built at Wabasha Street in the 1850s, and the street has been a major downtown thoroughfare since then. Despite its importance, Wabasha never developed a distinctive character in the manner of Nicollet or Hennepin Avenues in Minneapolis. Even so, Wabasha by the 1920s was a pleasingly crowded, modestly scaled street that offered many urban enticements.

This scene, chock-a-block with signs, shows the heart of Wabasha's shopping district between Sixth and Seventh. Visible at far left is a canopied entrance to Schuneman's Department Store, the largest retailer along the street. Smaller shops—clothing and shoe stores, jewelers, even a meat market (Friedman's, next to Schuneman's)—fill out both sides of the street to Seventh.

At Seventh, where the St. Francis Hotel–Orpheum Theater block had been built a few years before, a theater district of sorts began. It included the Astor, Strand (later Riviera), and Tower Theaters—all quite new at this time—as well as two older theaters, the Empress and the World (now Fitzgerald). Also nearby, on Seventh, was the city's greatest movie palace, the magnificent Capitol (later Paramount).

A picture taken in 1943 looking south along Wabasha from Eighth Street offers a better look at the theater district. The Strand (which received an art-deco facelift in 1933), the Tower (so named because of a picturesque feature of its design), and Riviera (featuring an Abbott and Costello extravaganza called *Hit the Ice*) are all in view. Note also the crowds waiting for streetcars. With wartime gas rationing in effect, such scenes were commonplace, since few people could afford to drive downtown. This area was to remain downtown's entertainment district until the 1970s, when the marquee lights went out one by one, extinguished by suburban competition.

The 1995 view north on Wabasha from Sixth shows a street shorn of virtually everything—including historic buildings and signs—that once made it interesting. The blank-walled brick box of Dayton's Department Store occupies a full block along the east side of Wabasha, while skyways siphon off much of the pedestrian traffic. To the north, all of the theaters (except for the Fitzgerald) are gone, although the colorful new Minnesota Children's Museum has brought a bit of youthful energy to a street (and a downtown) very much in need of that quality.

6   7   1   2   3   *1943*

Buildings and Places

1. Schuneman's Department Store (originally Kavanaugh Glass Block), Sixth and Wabasha, Edward P. Bassford, 1891–1964
2. St. Francis Hotel (later Seventh Place Apartments), Seventh and Wabasha, Buechner and Orth, 1916
3. Astor (later Riviera) Theater, Wabasha between Seventh and Ninth, Buechner and Orth, 1920–ca. 84
4. Boardman Hotel, Ninth and Wabasha, 1902–32
5. Trinity Evangelical Lutheran Church, Wabasha and Tilton, 1886–1952
6. Strand Theater, Eighth and Wabasha, 1922, 1933–78
7. Tower Theater, Wabasha between Seventh and Eighth, Toltz, King, and Day, 1921–59
8. Minnesota Children's Museum, Seventh (formerly Ninth) and Wabasha, James\Snow Architects and The Alliance, 1995
9. Dayton's Department Store, Sixth St. and Wabasha, Victor Gruen and Associates, 1963

1   2 3 4 5

2 8   9

Seventh Street

East from Wabasha Street, ca. 1922

Downtown St. Paul never had a real counterpart to Nicollet Avenue as a grand shopping street. Unlike Minneapolis—where major avenues such as Hennepin (entertainment), Nicollet (shopping), and Marquette (banking) had gravitated toward well-defined uses as early as 1900—St. Paul seemed to prefer a more scattershot approach. The city's major department stores, for example, were not nearly as tightly grouped as the big four along Nicollet in Minneapolis. Nonetheless Seventh Street—especially between Wabasha and Jackson—was the heart of downtown St. Paul's retail district for many years.

The view here shows Seventh at a time when St. Paul, Minneapolis, and other American cities were at the height of what might be called the Downtown Age. In the 1920s suburbs were still small and remote, the automobile did not yet dominate the urban landscape, and downtown—fed in St. Paul's case by a superb streetcar system—was the only place to go to work, to shop, and to be entertained.

A special retail map prepared in 1928 by the St. Paul Association of Public and Business Affairs provides one measure of downtown's vibrancy during this era. The map shows that downtown was home to sixty-three restaurants and diners, sixty clothing stores, twenty-four jewelers, twenty shoe stores, nineteen furniture stores, eleven theaters, and seven department stores, among many other businesses. A similar count today would be too depressing to contemplate.

It seems as though half of those businesses can be seen in the 1922 view along Seventh. Clothing and department stores, restaurants, hotels, and even a pair of theaters (the

1 2 3 4 5 6 *Ca. 1922*

Princess, on the left, and the Alhambra, on the right) are visible amid a wonderful cacophony of signs, lampposts, clocks, trolley wires, and other urban paraphernalia. Meanwhile well-dressed people throng the sidewalks. One of the more amazing features of this photograph is the sheer amount of haberdashery in evidence. In fact it appears that virtually everyone out and about on this summery day was wearing a hat (one of the few exceptions being the bareheaded boy next to the rather portly gentleman standing by the first pole at right).

Note also that most of the buildings along Seventh are quite old, many having been built in the 1880s. A photograph from about 1900, also looking east from Wabasha, reveals even older buildings, including a few constructed of wood. By 1922, however, these wooden structures were gone, done in by progress and by city fire codes that specified masonry construction in the downtown area. Even so, quite a few of the same buildings appear in both photographs, although by 1922 Seventh had seen at least two

Buildings and Places

1. Klein Block, Seventh and Wabasha, 1871–ca. 1930s
2. Princess Theater, Seventh near Wabasha, Mark Fitzpatrick, 1910–ca. 27 (closed)
3. Golden Rule (later Donaldson's) Department Store (now Golden Rule Building), Seventh and Robert, 1914 (Clarence H. Johnston), ca. 1985
4. Emporium Department Store (now Metro Square Building), Seventh and Robert, 1908 (Buechner and Orth), ca. 1970
5. Ryan Building (also known as Ryan Annex), Seventh and Robert, James J. Egan, 1887, 1896–1965
6. Alhambra Theater, Seventh near Wabasha, 1911–32 (closed)
7. Cardozo Building (now Bremer Tower), Seventh and Minnesota, 1932 (Ellerbe Architects), ca. 1980s
8. World Trade Center, Seventh and Wabasha, WZMH Group with Winsor Faricy Architects, 1987
9. Metropolitan Building (formerly Bremer Arcade), Seventh and Robert, ca. 1885, ca. 1915, 1960

8

1   5   *Ca. 1900*

significant new projects—the expanded Golden Rule and Emporium Department Stores, both of which occupied large buildings completed after 1910.

Seventh maintained much of its traditional character well into the 1950s and 1960s. Many of the historic buildings along Seventh were still standing in 1956, when another photographer took a view down the street from Wabasha. Most of the storefronts had been modernized by this time, however, and there had also been some new construction. One of the biggest additions was the handsome art-deco building erected at Seventh and Minnesota in 1933 by Cardozo's, a popular furniture store. Both the W. T. Grant Company and Woolworth's also had new stores on Seventh by 1956. Meanwhile the Golden Rule and the Emporium continued to hold down the corner of Seventh and Robert.

But change was already on the way. Southdale Mall in the Minneapolis suburb of Edina opened in 1956, and soon other large suburban malls began to capture much of the retail trade that had once gone downtown. The Emporium closed in 1967, and one by one the other shops and stores on Seventh departed or shut their doors. The Golden Rule (which in the 1960s became Donaldson's) moved to new quarters in Town Square in 1980. Its building, like the Emporium's, eventually became an office structure.

The street itself also underwent dramatic changes beginning in the late 1970s. Responding to a variety of development projects, the city decided to eliminate Seventh as a major artery and funnel most traffic a block north to Eighth. In typically confusing St. Paul fashion, Eighth was then renamed Seventh Street, while old Seventh became known as Seventh Place. The city also vacated a two-block stretch of old Seventh between Wabasha and Minnesota to make way for a pair of so-called "superblock" projects—Town Square in 1980 and the World Trade Center in 1987. Another part of Seventh Place, between St. Peter and Wabasha, was turned into a pedestrian mall, while the remainder of the street was devoted to angle parking.

A contemporary view from Wabasha east along old Seventh shows nothing except an entrance to the World Trade Center. Farther down Seventh Place, from near Minnesota, the view is not much better. The angled parking has turned the street into an elongated parking lot, and it is hard now to imagine that this was once the liveliest thoroughfare in St. Paul. What remains today is a ghost street, an intermittent shadow of its former self that serves only to highlight the misguided course of downtown planning in the 1970s and 1980s.

1956

1995

Sixth Street

East from Wabasha Street, 1922

This dramatic pair of photographs may cause viewers to blink their eyes, scratch their heads, and wonder what on earth happened to downtown St. Paul. The old picture shows downtown at its peak of vitality and urbanity. The world it depicts—dense, varied, strongly oriented toward the street—was largely a creation of the streetcar system that once dominated transportation in the Twin Cities (the record for annual trolley ridership—238 million—occurred in 1920). Since virtually all streetcar lines radiated from downtown, it was the place for business, social, and cultural activity.

Although Sixth was never downtown St. Paul's chief mercantile thoroughfare, the street nonetheless bustled with activity. The number of different businesses in view—more than twenty, judging from the signs—is astonishing by today's standards. Along this stretch of Sixth, shoppers could buy items as diverse as candy and coal, not to mention furs and pianos. A downtown visitor could also eat lunch, find a comfortable room (at the Ryan Hotel, its tower visible at left center), and be entertained at the Metropolitan Opera House, whose sign is barely visible just past the Exchange Bank Building (New York Life Insurance Company Building) on the right.

Yet this appealing photograph also hints at great changes to come. Automobiles and trucks clog the street, creating the sort of congestion that was to cause the

6 7 8 9 10 11

authors of the 1922 Plan of St. Paul to recommend extensive downtown street-widening. City leaders took this advice to heart, and over the years St. Paul's tight, European-style downtown was slowly transformed into a far more open, if less inviting, place.

Today the view down Sixth is among the bleakest in all of downtown. Much of this area fell prey to the huge Capital Centre redevelopment project beginning in the 1960s. Banal modern buildings gradually replaced the small brick storefronts that once lined the street, with results that were mostly disastrous. There is now virtually nothing of interest to look at along Sixth, which has become a sterile conduit for fast, one-way traffic. What pedestrian life remains has moved up to the skyways, as have most shops, and big blank walls stare out glumly over the street (a pernicious trend established by Dayton's Department Store, which in 1963 became the first modern building on this part of Sixth). Looking at these two pictures—one so lively, the other so dreary—it is hard not to mourn for the downtown of old.

Buildings and Places

1. Essex Building, 23 E. Sixth, ca. 1910–62
2. Ryan Hotel, Sixth and Robert, 1885–1962
3. Metropolitan Opera House, Sixth between Minnesota and Robert, Charles A. Reed and McElfatrick & Sons, 1890–1936
4. Exchange Bank (originally New York Life) Building, Sixth and Minnesota, Babb, Cook, and Willard, 1889–1967
5. Midland Building, Sixth and Wabasha, ca. 1910–67
6. Dayton's Department Store, Sixth and Cedar, 1963
7. Town Square, Sixth and Cedar, Skidmore, Owings, and Merrill, 1980
8. Minnesota Mutual Life Insurance Building (site of Ryan Hotel), Sixth and Robert, BWBR Architects, 1981
9. Galtier Plaza, Sixth and Sibley, Miller, Hanson, Westerbeck and Bell, 1986
10. Norwest Center Building and ramp, Sixth and Minnesota (site of New York Life Building), Grover Dimond Associates, 1971
11. Capital Centre Building, Sixth and Wabasha (site of Midland Building), Grover Dimond Associates, 1973

Cedar Street

North from Fourth Street, ca. 1905

These panoramic views up Cedar Street show the enormous changes in downtown's central core wrought by ninety years of progress. With only two exceptions—the State Capitol and Central Presbyterian Church—everything in the 1905 view was gone by 1995, a transformation that belies St. Paul's reputation for preserving its past. Yet there is nothing extraordinary about this wholesale replacement of buildings, since virtually every other American downtown has followed the same course.

The historic photograph was taken from one of St. Paul's great early skyscrapers—the ten-story Globe Building (1887) at the southwest corner of Fourth and Cedar. The picture demonstrates how modest the scale of downtown was at this time, with three- and four-story buildings predominating. All of these low buildings in the foreground make the recently completed State Capitol seem especially splendid, a Renaissance prince presiding over the city.

The Capitol, however, is not the only new building visible in this photograph. The period just after the turn of the century saw much construction downtown as both government and business sought to replace or update outmoded buildings from the boom years of the 1880s. (In fact rubble visible in the street near Central Presbyterian is probably connected to construction of the YMCA at Ninth and Cedar, completed in 1907 and razed in the 1980s.) New banks and hotels were especially common during this time, and one of each can be seen here—the American National Bank Building (1905) and the Frederic Hotel (1903).

The new Capitol also replaced a building from the 1880s—the second State Capitol, whose domed tower rises just to the left of Cass Gilbert's white marble palace. But it would be another twenty-five years before the city's other major nineteenth-century monument to government, the St. Paul City Hall–Ramsey County Courthouse (at far left), met a similar fate.

The 1995 photograph was shot from atop the Degree of Honor Building, which replaced the Globe after it was torn down in 1959. The new view shows that buildings from every decade after World War II, all in one variation or another of the modernist style, now line Cedar. These new structures are much taller and larger than their predecessors, which means there are far fewer buildings along Cedar than was once the case. One result of this development is visual boredom: there simply are not as many different kinds of buildings to look at as there were ninety years ago. Cedar has also acquired the usual complement of skyways, plus one truly egregious folly of modern planning—the Norwest Center "superblock" ramp between Fifth and Sixth that blocks views of the Capitol while creating a dark, unpleasant cave for pedestrians below.

7   8 3 4   9   10

Buildings and Places

1. St. Paul City Hall–Ramsey County Courthouse, Fourth and Cedar, 1889–1933
2. Second Minnesota State Capitol, Tenth and Wabasha, LeRoy S. Buffington, 1883–1938
3. State Capitol, 1905
4. Central Presbyterian Church, Cedar and Exchange, Warren H. Hayes, 1889
5. Frederic Hotel, Fifth and Cedar, 1903–61
6. American National Bank Building, Fifth and Cedar, Alfred Wheeler, 1905, ca. 1907–71
7. St. Paul Pioneer Press Building (originally Minnesota Mutual Insurance), Fourth and Cedar, Ellerbe Associates, 1955
8. World Trade Center, Seventh and Cedar, 1987
9. Piper Jaffray Tower, Seventh and Cedar, 1980
10. Norwest Center Building and ramp, Sixth and Cedar, 1971

St. Peter, Washington, and Market Streets

South from Seventh Street, ca. 1925

Unlike much of downtown St. Paul, the Rice Park area has managed to retain a good deal of its historic architecture, as these photographs demonstrate. The great north tower of Landmark Center dominates both pictures, and several other familiar monuments can also be seen, including the Hamm Building, the Lowry Medical Arts Building, and the St. Paul Hotel.

While the larger buildings here have survived seventy years of growth and change, the smaller ones have not.

Thus the old Degree of Honor Building is gone, as is the original St. Paul Orpheum Theater, where all the famous vaudevillians once performed. Gone too are the Euclid (later Grand) Hotel and an intriguing little building (with the "Weitzman's Clever Clothes" sign) that occupied the wedge-shaped block between Market and Washington near the Federal Courts Building. (What the two gents posed in front of this building are up to is anyone's guess, although one of them appears to be a fire or police official.)

The building went by a number of names over the years but was often simply called the Flatiron Block, a generic moniker bestowed on almost any building occupying a wedge-shaped site. While hardly as grand as the most famous Flatiron Building of all (in New York City at Twenty-third and Broadway), St. Paul's version was well known locally, serving for many years as home to the city's Union Bus Depot. The depot occupied the south (and wider) part of the building along Sixth from 1923 until about 1954, when a new depot opened a few blocks away.

What is especially nice about the old photograph is how sharply buildings define and contain the converging streets. And even though these buildings are of varying sizes and types, they use a similar palette of materials—almost all are some combination of brick and stone—so that everything blends together. It is easy to imagine strolling through this part of St. Paul in the 1920s and finding something interesting to look at on almost every block.

The contemporary view, despite such significant additions as the St. Paul Companies Building and Landmark Tower, is less satisfying. Parking lots and plazas (including an expensive but largely useless one in front of Landmark Center) have punched gaping holes in the tight old streetscape, and Washington has been cut off at Sixth to make way for a small traffic circle serving the St. Paul Companies. Much of the street-level retailing is also long gone. Still this section of downtown has evolved reasonably well, its major monuments intact, and it remains a pleasant and inviting corner of the city.

Buildings and Places

1. Hamm Building, St. Peter between Sixth and Seventh, Toltz, King, and Day, 1920
2. St. Paul Hotel, Fifth and St. Peter, 1910 (Reed and Stem), 1981, 1990
3. Armstrong (later Degree of Honor) Building, Sixth and St. Peter, Reed and Stem, 1893–1975
4. Orpheum (later President) Theater (only rear part visible), Fifth and St. Peter, Kees and Colburn, 1906–39
5. Flatiron Block (Union Bus Depot), Sixth between St. Peter, Market, and Washington, ca. 1900–59
6. Federal Courts Building (now Landmark Center), Fifth between Market and Washington, supervising architect of the U.S. Treasury, 1892, 1902
7. Euclid (Grand) Hotel, Sixth and Washington, ca. 1900–ca. 71
8. Landmark Tower (originally Amhoist Building), Fourth and St. Peter, BRW Architects, 1983
9. St. Paul Companies, Sixth and Washington, Kohn Pedersen Fox and The Alliance, 1991

Fifth Street

East from Auditorium Street, ca. 1920

Urban redevelopment should, at the minimum, be a zero-sum proposition in which the benefits of the new offset the loss of the old. It does not always work out that way, of course, but this pair of views reveals what on the whole has been a fair deal for St. Paul. The new buildings, especially the Ordway Music Theatre, have been strong additions to the city, even though their construction came at the cost of several fine old structures (as well as one street).

The historic photograph shows an architectural ensemble that was actually quite new at the time. Except for the three-story, Italianate-style building in front of the St. Paul Hotel, almost all of the nonresidential buildings date from after the turn of the century. The oldest is the St. Paul Auditorium, built in 1907 and widely hailed for its flexible design, which allowed a variety of seating arrangements for different kinds of events. Like almost all public buildings of this period, the auditorium was also wonderfully urbane, using the prevailing neoclassical idiom to create a dignified presence on the street. The St. Paul YWCA, directly across from the auditorium, offers similar virtues. The YWCA building, incidentally, replaced a house occupied for many years by the parents of Archbishop John Ireland, one of St. Paul's great religious leaders.

The two ornate Victorians next to the YWCA were among quite a number of old houses—generally subdivided into apartments or used as rooming houses—that once stood along West Fifth. Their numbers began to dwindle

Buildings and Places

1. Charles E. Smith house, Fifth and Auditorium, ca. 1885
2. St. Paul YWCA, Fifth near Auditorium, Clarence H. Johnston, 1912–61
3. St. Paul Fire & Marine Insurance Co. (later St. Paul Companies), Fifth and Washington, Louis Lockwood, 1909–ca. 59
4. St. Paul Hotel, Fifth and St. Peter, 1910, 1981, 1990
5. St. Paul Auditorium, Fifth between Washington and Auditorium, Reed and Stem, 1907–82
6. St. Paul Companies, Fifth and Washington, 1961 (Childs and Smith), 1981 (Ellerbe Associates), 1992 (Kohn Pedersen Fox)
7. Landmark Tower (originally Amhoist Building), Fourth and St. Peter, 1983
8. Ordway Music Theatre, Fifth and Washington, Benjamin Thompson and Associates, 1985
9. Roy Wilkins Auditorium, Fifth between Washington and Seventh, 1932 (Ellerbe Architects), 1983

steadily, however, as more and more businesses, such as the Cadillac dealer at right, located in this part of downtown after about 1910.

Not surprisingly, the houses are gone from the modern view, as is the old YWCA, torn down long ago for expansion by the growing St. Paul Companies. Auditorium (originally Franklin) Street has also vanished, one of many ghost streets that haunt St. Paul. The other major change here involves the auditorium, which received an addition

(now called the Roy Wilkins Auditorium) in 1932. The Wilkins arena remains in use as part of the St. Paul Civic Center, but the original auditorium (later called Stem Hall) fell to the wrecker in 1982 to make way for a new civic monument—the Ordway Theatre. Meanwhile the St. Paul Hotel, refurbished and wisely reoriented toward Rice Park, continues to preside gracefully over a part of downtown where the old and the new have managed to blend quite nicely.

Robert Street

North from Third, Fourth, Fifth, and Sixth Streets, ca. 1912

This remarkable series of photographs shows one of St. Paul's principal downtown streets at a crucial point in its history. Not long after these views were taken, the city widened Robert by twenty feet from Third (now Kellogg Boulevard) all the way to University Avenue at a cost of $1 million. That seems like a modest sum considering that the project entailed slicing off the fronts of many old buildings on the west side of the street and erecting new façades. The new Robert became seventy-five feet wide (including sidewalks), changing its look forever.

The four views here convey a sense of how densely built and crowded much of downtown St. Paul was at the turn of the century. They also show how Robert's urban character changed subtly from block to block. A stroll down the street in 1912 must have been like walking through a suite of connecting rooms, all related yet each with its own style and mood.

Ca. 1912   **1**   **2**   **3**

1   **4   5**

The sequence begins at Third, where Robert appears to be a street already past its best days. Cheap bars, faded hotels, and small wholesaling businesses cluster around the intersection, many of them housed in brick or stone buildings from the 1860s and 1870s. Bracketing this view are two such elderly architectural citizens—a brick structure on the left (housing a hotel and liquor store) and the U.S. Hotel on the right.

2   10   11   12 4 5   2

At Fourth, Robert assumes a more stately character, largely because of the big office buildings overlooking the intersection. To the right is the sixteen-story Pioneer (originally Pioneer Press) Building, in 1912 the city's tallest skyscraper. Across from it is the National German-American Bank. Both the bank and its building were soon to disappear, however, consumed by the larger Merchants Bank in 1915.

The street becomes much more oriented to shopping at Fifth, where pedestrian activity is at its peak amid a jungle of signs. Also in view are numerous workers—an umbrella-shaded teamster on his delivery wagon, a street sweeper, a policeman directing traffic, and even a fellow on a dangling scaffold (upper left) who seems to be cleaning windows.

The final view, at Sixth, showcases one of the city's

great monuments—the Ryan Hotel. Photographs from a distance seldom do justice to the Ryan, and only when the hotel is seen up close, as it is here, does its ornamental exuberance become fully apparent. Note also the banner on the third floor of the hotel touting the candidacy of one E. T. Young for governor. The voters, unfortunately, failed to respond and E. T. was called home. Across from the Ryan is Mannheimer Brothers Department Store, while just up the street at Seventh are two of its biggest competitors—the Emporium and the Golden Rule.

Although automobile traffic in these pictures is sparse—by one estimate there were only eleven hundred cars in St. Paul in 1910—the numbers would soon increase dramatically. In 1920, for example, a count showed fifty-five thousand motor vehicles entering or leaving downtown

Ca. 1912   6

Buildings and Places

1. National German-American Bank, Fourth and Robert, George Wirth, 1885–1913
2. Pioneer (originally Pioneer Press) Building, Fourth and Robert, 1889 (Solon Beman), 1910, 1983
3. U.S. Hotel, Third and Robert, ca. 1870–1952
4. Manhattan (later Empire) Building, Fifth and Robert, Clarence H. Johnston, 1891
5. Endicott on Robert Building, Robert between Fourth and Fifth, Gilbert and Taylor, 1890
6. Ryan Hotel, Sixth and Robert, James J. Egan, 1885–1962
7. Mannheimer Brothers Building, Sixth and Robert, Reed and Stem, 1893–1966
8. Golden Rule Department Store (now Golden Rule Building), Seventh and Robert, 1914, ca. 1985
9. Emporium Department Store (now Metro Square Building), Seventh and Robert, ca. 1908, ca. 1970
10. Kellogg Square Apartments, Fourth and Robert, 1972
11. Merchants Bank Building (now First Bank of St. Paul), Fourth and Robert, Jarvis Hunt, 1915
12. Minnesota Mutual Life Insurance Building (site of Ryan Hotel), Sixth and Robert, 1981

during one twelve-hour period. This growing vehicular problem, exacerbated when streetcars clogged traffic on narrow streets, was among the reasons why the city decided to widen Robert in 1913.

The project proved to be a disappointment because, even at its new width, Robert remained too narrow in the eyes of city planners. "The cross section of the street was not sufficient to provide for six lanes of traffic," longtime St. Paul city planner George Herrold wrote, "and instead of erecting new buildings along the widened side of the street, new fronts were put on very old buildings and then rents were increased." As a result, the overriding goal of the project, which was to improve traffic flow and thereby make the street more commercially viable, was never met to everyone's satisfaction. Property values did indeed rise

after the widening, but they failed to increase as much as building owners had hoped.

Two 1995 views (from Fourth and Sixth) show that much of the street remains at the 1913 width, although Robert has been broadened yet again on some blocks. Alas, the delightful melange of buildings once found along Robert has all but vanished, as has most of the street's retailing. Even so, Robert retains a few pleasures. The Pioneer Building, with its splendid light court, is still going strong. Its neighbors—the Endicott on Robert and Empire Buildings—have also been spared, with the result that this block offers the finest ensemble of nineteenth-century commercial architecture in all of downtown. The new architecture, on the other hand, is uniformly sterile and has helped drain the street of much of its old vitality.

Third Street

East from Robert Street, 1928

West from Jackson Street, 1928

For much of the nineteenth century, Third Street (now Kellogg Boulevard) was downtown St. Paul's main commercial artery. Built at the edge of the bluff overlooking the Mississippi River, Third was by 1880 home to many of the city's largest retail and wholesale businesses. As such it gradually became an outdoor museum of early Victorian commercial architecture, with a fine array of small brick and stone buildings dating as far back as the 1850s. By the mid-1880s, however, St. Paul's major retailers began to relocate along Sixth and Seventh Streets, while wholesalers concentrated in Lowertown. As a result Third lost much of its cachet and gradually came to be seen as an old, blighted part of town, much like the Gateway District in Minneapolis.

Very narrow even by St. Paul standards, Third originally was only forty-five feet wide, although it was expanded to fifty-seven feet in 1872 by the simple expedient of lopping off porches from buildings along the street. Third retained

| 4 | 5 | 2 | 6 | 7 |

its narrowness, and its almost Old World look, right through the 1920s, as these two photographs from 1928 attest.

The view east from Robert shows a compact array of buildings, among them the U.S. Hotel (far left), where Jesse James and his gang are reputed to have convened before their disastrous Northfield bank robbery of 1876. Note also the small Mobil gas station at left, the large Coca-Cola sign painted on the building nearby, and the lack of parking meters (which did not arrive in St. Paul until the 1930s). The only twentieth-century building visible (and the only structure in this view that survives today) is the Union Depot concourse, which can be seen crossing Third in the center of the photograph.

A photograph west from Jackson shows that the street's character did not change much as it went uphill toward the center of downtown. Here again, rather tired-looking Victorians line the street, with occasional holes marking the location of vanished buildings. At far left is an old stone building that originally housed one of the city's pioneer businesses—the St. Paul Companies. The insurance firm had moved elsewhere downtown by this time, as had many of the other large companies once located on Third.

Buildings and Places

1. U.S. Hotel, Third and Robert, ca. 1870–1952
2. Union Depot concourse, Third between Sibley and Wacouta, Charles S. Frost, 1923
3. St. Paul Fire & Marine Insurance Co. (later Volkszeitung) Building, Third and Jackson, Monroe and Romaine Sheire, 1870–1928
4. Warren E. Burger Federal Building, Kellogg and Robert, Walter Butler Co. with Haarstick, Lundgren, and Associates, 1966
5. Minnesota Telecenter (KTCA-TV), Kellogg and Jackson, Hammel, Green, and Abrahamson, 1988
6. U.S. Post Office, Kellogg and Jackson, Bassingdale, Holabird, and Root, 1934
7. Ramsey County Government Center East (originally Farwell, Ozmun, and Kirk Co.), Kellogg and Robert, 1906 (Louis Lockwood), ca. 1970s, 1995
8. Kellogg Mall Park, 1932, 1989
9. St. Paul Radisson (originally Hilton) Hotel, Kellogg and Wabasha, William B. Tabler, 1966
10. Saturn School (formerly YWCA), Kellogg and Minnesota, 1961 (Grover Dimond Associates), 1988
11. Kellogg Square Apartments, Kellogg and Robert, Convention Center Architects and Engineers, 1972

3

Businesses still visible along Third in these photographs include the Anderson Employment Agency (right), inexpensive restaurants like the Bluebird and Fargo Cafes (also on the right), bargain-priced hotels like the U.S., and numerous small companies dealing in everything from awnings and tents to signs. Although Third seems to have remained reasonably busy at this time, the old photographs leave little doubt that it was far from being the best part of town.

As it turned out, 1928 was to be a key year in Third

Street's history. City visionaries had for many years complained that buildings on the south side of Third blocked any bluff-top view of the river. The deteriorating condition of the old buildings along the street, as well as the traffic problems caused by its narrowness, also spurred calls to action. In 1928 a $15 million city bond project (which included $4 million for the present city hall–county courthouse) finally provided the money to rebuild and widen Third from Lowertown to Seven Corners. Over the next eight years, forty-three buildings along Third and nearby

Bench Street (now Second) were demolished. Out of this massive urban renewal project came today's Kellogg Boulevard (named after St. Paul statesman Frank B. Kellogg). This project also produced the Kellogg Mall Park between Robert and Wabasha.

Today the view east and west along Kellogg from Robert shows a much more spacious urban environment than existed in 1928. New buildings have replaced all of the old structures that once lined the north side of the street (which is where old Third was located), while most of the south side is open to the river. It is pleasant to think how Third, had it been preserved, might have become the center of a lively St. Paul "old town." But so foresighted an act of preservation would have been a true urban miracle.

The transformation of Third into Kellogg produced the sort of ambivalent outcome that often characterizes urban renewal. Although St. Paul lost an important part of its historic fabric as a result of the project, it gained much-needed new development and a pleasing view of the river from which it sprang.

Fourth Street

East from near Jackson Street, ca. 1910

Despite being stained and crinkled with age, this photograph offers an excellent view of East Fourth Street at the turn of the century. What makes the view particularly interesting is that it demonstrates how much of the "historic" Lowertown of today is built on the ruins of an earlier generation of buildings.

Several of the city's largest office buildings from the early 1880s are visible here, including three at the intersection of Fourth and Jackson: the old First National Bank, the Davidson Block, and the Gilfillan Block. The Davidson Block, named for St. Paul real estate mogul William Davidson, actually began life in 1876 as a five-story building (complete with one of the earliest passenger elevators in the Twin Cities) but was cut to four floors after a fire in 1880.

Farther down Fourth, at Sibley Street, is the Sherman Hotel. Its proprietor for many years was Marshall Sherman, who won a Congressional Medal of Honor at Gettysburg fighting with the legendary First Minnesota Volunteer Regiment and later lost a leg at Deep Bottom Run in Virginia. Past the hotel on the other side of the street is a much newer building—the seven-story Lindeke, Warner,

| 8 | 9 | 10 | 5 | 11 | 12 |

and Sons warehouse completed in 1908. Closing off the view down Fourth is the Northern Pacific Building, erected in 1883, the same year that the railroad completed its transcontinental line to the Pacific.

This part of Fourth was a busy retail and wholesaling district in 1910, and numerous delivery wagons make their way along the streets. Several streetcars can also be seen plying what was the oldest motorized line in the Twin Cities, first used in 1888 by steam-powered cable cars.

The 1995 view reveals that little from the earlier photograph survives. Some of the old buildings, in fact, have been gone for fifty years or more. Change came early to Lowertown because advances in building technology (especially the development of concrete framing) led to the construction of many new warehouses after 1900. It is these buildings that now form the heart of the Lowertown Historic District.

The opening of James J. Hill's mammoth Railroad and Bank Building in 1916 and the Union Depot a few years later also transformed East Fourth, as did major projects in the 1960s and 1980s. But as the downtown "trolley" in the 1995 photograph demonstrates, St. Paul continues to be nostalgic about its past, even if the city has not always found ways to preserve it.

Buildings and Places

1. First National Bank (later Hackney Building), Fourth and Jackson, Denslow W. Millard, 1885–1941
2. Davidson Block, Fourth and Jackson, Edward P. Bassford, 1876, 1880–ca. 1914
3. Lindeke, Warner, and Sons Co. (later Toni Co.), Fourth and Rosabel (now Wall), Louis Lockwood, 1908–ca. 70
4. Northern Pacific Building, Broadway and Prince, B. L. Gilbert, 1883–1929
5. St. Paul Rubber Co. (now Lowertown Commons), Fourth and Broadway, 1905, 1986
6. Sherman Hotel, Fourth and Sibley, ca. 1860s, 1873, 1879–ca. 1916
7. Gilfillan Block, Fourth and Jackson, Edward P. Bassford, 1882–ca. 1940
8. First Trust Center (formerly Railroad and Bank Building), Fourth and Jackson, 1916 (Charles S. Frost), ca. 1987
9. Army Corps of Engineers Centre (formerly Gordon and Ferguson Co.), Fourth and Sibley, 1913 (Clarence H. Johnston), 1994
10. Gillette Co. (site of Northern Pacific Building), Broadway at Fourth, 1969
11. St. Paul Community Services Building, Fourth and Jackson, 1989
12. Warren E. Burger Federal Building, Fourth and Robert, 1966

Seventh Street

East from near Sibley Street, 1931

The surveyors who laid out downtown St. Paul beginning in the 1840s were notoriously stingy when it came to streets. Most of the streets in St. Paul Proper and the nearby plats that quickly followed were just sixty feet wide (including sidewalks), a modest dimension that was to bedevil city engineers for decades to come. Although this narrowness gave St. Paul's streets an undeniable European-style charm, it led to all sorts of traffic problems, especially after streetcars and automobiles began to compete seriously for road space after the turn of the century.

To remedy this historic misfortune, St. Paul city government undertook numerous street widening schemes over the years. One of the largest and costliest of these ventures was the widening of Robert Street in 1913 (see page 120). The city launched an even larger project around 1930, when Seventh, Eighth, and Ninth Streets were widened at a cost of $4.6 million. This photograph documents one section of the work on Seventh.

The expansion of Seventh from sixty to eighty-six feet was accomplished by lopping off building fronts on the north side of the street. Most of the architectural surgery had already been performed by the time of this picture, and the old buildings with their new (and, it appears, mostly art-deco) façades can be seen amid the rubble and

disarray of construction. Streetcar tracks also had to be moved to accommodate the widened street, and that work is under way as well. One can only imagine the disruption this massive public works project must have caused to the businesses along East Seventh, which remained a busy—if somewhat faded—commercial district in 1931.

The 1995 view shows that St. Paul's tinkering with East Seventh did not end with the big 1931 widening project. In the 1980s, the street was widened once again (only slightly) and also realigned west of Sibley to follow the old route of Eighth Street. At about the same time, most of the buildings along the north side of the street were cleared away in hopes of attracting new development. As of 1995, however, this "development" consisted exclusively of parking lots. Nonetheless a few old-timers like the Gopher Bar and Cafe have managed to survive.

Meanwhile the south side of Seventh—now part of the Lowertown Historic District—has remained surprisingly solid, its row of old Victorians still holding out against the assault of time.

Buildings and Places

1. Union Gospel Mission, Seventh and Wacouta, 1910, 1927–80
2. Commercial building (Gopher Bar and Cafe), 241 E. Seventh, ca. 1870s, 1931
3. O'Connor Block, 264–266 E. Seventh, Emil Ulrici, 1887
4. Constans Block (later Butwinicks Furniture Co.), 224–240 E. Seventh, Augustus Gauger, 1884

Seventh Street

East from near Rosabel (Wall) Street, 1944

The eastern edge of Lowertown has gone through three distinct lives since the founding of St. Paul. Initially this part of Lowertown, extending from Broadway Street to Trout Brook Valley, was mostly residential and included some of the largest houses in the city. But the mansions built in the 1850s, 1860s, and 1870s did not last because railroad expansion through the valley in the 1880s brought noise, smoke, and the inevitable encroachment of industry. By 1900 the area had already begun its second life as a commercial, industrial, and warehousing district.

A 1944 picture, taken from the roof of what is today the Pioneer Vending Company at 266 East Seventh, shows this second stage of the neighborhood's life. The photograph offers a sweeping view of East Seventh all the way from Olive Street (which crosses just behind the Dad's Root Beer sign) to the summit of Dayton's Bluff. On the north side of Seventh, small commercial buildings predominate, among them several housing auto-related businesses. Farther north, on Eighth, is a six-story structure occupied by the St. Paul Terminal Warehouse Company. A Soo Line freight terminal can also be seen nearby, while the Great Northern freight terminal is just out of view to the left (see page 134). The south side of Seventh is more industrial in character and includes such firms as the Model Steam Laundry and the Kenny Boiler Manufacturing Company.

East Seventh was, of course, a major streetcar route and had been since the 1880s, when the street was regraded

1   6   7

and rebuilt all the way from downtown to the top of the bluff. This gigantic project, known as the Seventh Street fill, cost $140,000 (a princely sum in those days) and produced at least one engineering marvel—the rare helicoidal stone arches from 1883 that carry Seventh across Swede Hollow.

A view from the same rooftop today shows the area in its third life, as a mixed office and commercial zone close to Interstate 94. Construction of the freeway in the 1960s changed the neighborhood forever. The industrial plants south of Seventh vanished, as did many of the old brick buildings on the north side of the street. A section of Seventh itself was also moved by curving it to the north to accommodate a complicated interchange with U.S. Highway 52 (the Lafayette Freeway). Meanwhile many of the warehouses and railroad buildings north of Seventh were converted into offices, mainly for state agencies.

Buildings and Places

1. St. Paul Terminal Warehouse Co. (now Minnesota Department of Human Services), Eighth and Lafayette Rd., ca. 1910, ca. 1980s
2. Soo Line freight terminal, Seventh and Neill, ca. 1918–ca. 80
3. St. John's Hospital, Sixth and Mounds Blvd., 1910, ca. 1960s–88 (hospital closed)
4. Sixth Street viaduct, across Trout Brook Valley and Swede Hollow, ca. 1890–1960; new bridge, ca. 1967
5. Model Steam Laundry, Sixth and Pine, ca. 1890s–ca. 1960
6. Metropolitan State University New Main (site of St. John's Hospital), Sixth and Mounds Blvd., Bentz/Thompson/Rietow, 1994
7. Interstate 94, opened 1967

Great Northern Freight Terminal

Northwest from Eighth and Olive Streets, 1918

Mississippi Street

North from near Mt. Airy Street, 1917

ong before the interstate highway system appeared, railroads were among the great shapers of the American urban landscape. In St. Paul, headquarters of James J. Hill's Great Northern and other lines, railroads had an especially profound impact on the development of the city. Here are three historic views of one of the largest rail projects of its era in St. Paul: construction of the Great Northern Railway's Eighth Street freight terminal. Amazingly it was undertaken just as the railroads were beginning another huge building scheme—the Union Depot complex on Fourth Street—less than a mile away.

The Eighth Street project involved clearing more than six square blocks of land in Lowertown to make way for

1   2   3   *1918*

2   9

the terminal and its approaches. The site—roughly bounded by Pine, John, Eighth, and Grove Streets—was historic urban ground, a residential neighborhood platted in the 1850s that had once been home to some of St. Paul's leading families. But the neighborhood's character changed as a result of railroad incursions beginning in the late nineteenth century. A tornado in August 1904, the same one that knocked down part of the Smith Avenue High Bridge (see page 164), dealt another blow to the neighborhood's fortunes. By 1917 the area had evolved into a rather decrepit part of town that still contained a scattering of fine old houses. It is a measure of the Great Northern's financial and legal muscle at this time that all of this land was cleared and the new terminal constructed in only three years.

Two views from Eighth demonstrate the scope of the project. The first photograph, from November 1918, shows the nearly finished terminal building at Eighth and Pine,

with boxcars lined up beside it. Another view from the same time depicts the area immediately to the east between Olive and John Streets. Here a large swath of land, some of it not yet cleared of rubble from demolished buildings, awaits the next stage of construction.

Note also the church towers in the vicinity. This neighborhood was home to several of the city's most historic churches. Among them was the first St. Mary's Catholic Church. A limestone landmark from 1867, the old St. Mary's survived for fifty years as a lumber company storage building after the congregation moved to a new church in 1922.

On its northern end, the freight terminal project also required some serious earth moving. To bring construction equipment to the site, a track was laid along the east side of Mississippi Street in 1917. One flank of Williams Hill, an early residential district, was carved back in the process. Several buildings along Mississippi were demolished as

Ca. 1918   4   5   6   7

well. A 1917 photograph, which almost looks as though it might have been taken in some dusty old western town, shows the early stages of this work. Note that a grade has already been prepared along the side of the hill and that construction of the track itself has begun up ahead. At this time Mississippi Street still functioned as a major thoroughfare north out of downtown, with a streetcar line and clusters of commercial buildings.

Today the railroad tracks that molded so much of St. Paul's landscape have slowly receded like the glaciers of ten thousand years ago, and the terminal complex is long gone. Although modern construction and the loss of nearby buildings have made it impossible to duplicate the angle of the old photographs, a contemporary ground-level view gives some sense of what has happened to the terminal site. The front part of the Great Northern building at Eighth and Pine still stands and is used for offices. The rest

8   *1917*

of the site, however, is occupied by a large warehouse built after removal of the railroad tracks. Interstate highways also cut through this area in the 1960s, so that the old terminal site is now within easy eye shot of one of the major causes of its demise.

Mississippi Street has been transformed as well, and a salvage yard has replaced the scene in the old photograph. The west side of Mississippi now abuts Interstate 35E, while to the east the original Williams Hill is no more—chewed away for its gravel and then reconstituted into mounds of construction debris. The city hopes to clear away this debris and eventually turn the site into an industrial park.

So goes the history of one of St. Paul's most intriguing places, where mansions, churches, businesses, streets, railroad tracks, and even an entire hill have come and gone in less than a century and a half. One can only imagine what the next 150 years might bring.

Buildings and Places

1. First Baptist Church, Ninth and Wacouta, William W. Boyington, 1875
2. Great Northern Railway freight terminal, Eighth and Pine, 1918, ca. 1967
3. Emmanuel German Evangelical Church, Eleventh and Pine, 1863–1919
4. First Swedish Evangelical Lutheran (later First Lutheran) Church, John and Woodward, 1867, ca. 1880–1918
5. Samuel D. Flagg house (later rectory of St. Mary's Catholic Church), Ninth and John, ca. 1870–ca. 1920s
6. St. Mary's Catholic Church, Ninth and Lafayette, Augustus F. Knight, 1867–1922, ca. 1970
7. St. Mary's School, Ninth and Lafayette, 1887–ca. 1920s
8. Williams Hill
9. Space Center, Inc., warehouse, Eighth and Olive, 1968

8

Rail Yards

East from Union Depot, 1926

Here are two scenes that illustrate, with uncommon clarity, the decline of railroading in St. Paul since the 1920s, when the Age of Steam was still going strong. The historic photograph shows the sprawling Union Depot yards that once filled much of the Trout Brook Valley east of downtown. These yards, which handled extensive passenger and freight traffic, formed a vast Y where tracks coming in from Trout Brook Valley and Swede Hollow connected with others along the banks of the Mississippi River. All told, more than thirty sets of tracks—used by ten railroads—are visible.

The photograph was probably taken from atop one of the canopies that sheltered passengers as they boarded or disembarked from trains behind the depot, which was actually quite new in 1926. Built between 1917 and 1923, it replaced an earlier station that had burned ten years before.

The scale of the Union Depot project was truly epic. It required demolition of several blocks' worth of old warehouses and hotels, construction of the new depot and concourse, and the building of a huge new platform to lift tracks above the flood-prone Mississippi. (The existing Robert Street Bridge, built in 1926, also resulted from this project, since the old bridge would not have provided enough clearance for the newly elevated tracks below.) It is doubtful that any private consortium would even consider a project on this scale today. But railroads once had the money and power to move mountains (literally, in some cases), and the Union Depot project was to be one of their last great enterprises in St. Paul.

1

2

3   4   5

Today the railroads in St. Paul and elsewhere are a shrunken remnant of their former selves, and the ghost traces of abandoned railbeds are now a common sight throughout America. As for the old Union Depot yards, a 1995 view from the depot's vacant concourse pretty much says it all. Roads, freeways, bridges, and a U.S. Postal Service parking lot (built on the platform that once brought trains to the depot) have largely replaced the old railroad yards, although a few tracks still run near the river beside Warner Road. Even though the railroads remain, much of the world they made—as these photographs demonstrate—is gone forever.

Buildings and Places

1. Third Street (now Kellogg Blvd.) viaduct, over Trout Brook–Phalen Creek Valley, ca. 1890–1929; second bridge, 1931–82; third bridge, 1983
2. Van Buren School, Bates Ave. and Conway St., 1882 (William H. Willcox), 1887 (Willcox and Johnston)–1975
3. Metropolitan State University New Main, Sixth St. and Mounds Blvd., 1994
4. Lafayette Bridge, across Mississippi River, 1968
5. Warner Road Park (beneath Lafayette Bridge), 1994

Downtown and Riverfront

West from Dayton's Bluff, ca. 1894

Downtown St. Paul's topography, which is basically that of an amphitheater ringed by hills, made it an ideal subject for panoramic views from a variety of vantage points. The vista from the high hills east of downtown—today's Dayton's Bluff and Mounds Park neighborhoods—was especially popular in the nineteenth century, perhaps because it showed off the city's railroad network so well.

Tracks dominate the foreground of the 1894 photograph, spreading out through the gigantic yards that once filled the old Trout Brook–Phalen Creek Valley at downtown's eastern edge. This valley, offering an easy natural grade down to the river, became the city's great railroad corridor beginning in the 1870s. On the far side of the tracks is Lowertown, which then extended much farther east than it does today. A number of Lowertown's major monuments are visible here, including the old Great Northern Building and the Farwell, Ozmun, and Kirk (later Tilsner Box Company) warehouse, both of which still stand. Note also the old bluff-top limestone quarry at right and the handsome brick house near the top of the cliff.

Before being transformed by millions of cubic yards of fill obtained by leveling Baptist Hill (now the site of Mears Park) in the 1870s, Trout Brook–Phalen Creek Valley was known as "the bottomless bog." During spring floods, this swampy valley often backed up with river water. An earlier picture, taken from above Carver's Cave at a point somewhat north of the 1894 photograph, shows just such a backup beneath the low bluffs where Interstate 94 now runs. Dating from about 1885, this picture also highlights the extent of the city's railroad industry. Boxcars by the dozens are in view, as are several freight stations, where material such as lumber—large piles are visible—could be unloaded or loaded for shipment to its final destination.

Today's view underscores the changes wrought by a century of progress. Virtually all of the buildings visible in the old photographs are gone, and many of the railroad tracks have disappeared as well. The one constant in this world of flux is the Mississippi, which still sweeps gracefully past downtown before making its big turn south. A new park off Warner Road has added some welcome greenery to the scene, while trees now cover bluffs once stripped bare by railroad builders. Nature, in this case, has proved to be St. Paul's most enduring presence.

5   3   *Ca. 1885*

Buildings and Places

1. St. Paul, Minneapolis, and Manitoba (later Great Northern) Office Building, Third (Kellogg Blvd.) and Broadway, James Brodie, 1887, 1900
2. Farwell, Ozmun, and Kirk warehouse (now Tilsner Artists Cooperative), Kellogg Blvd. and Broadway, 1894 (Edward P. Bassford), 1994
3. Second State Capitol, Tenth and Wabasha, 1883–1938
4. Third Street (Kellogg Blvd.) viaduct, ca. 1890–1929; second bridge, 1931–82; third bridge, 1983
5. Assumption Catholic Church, Seventh (formerly Ninth) near St. Peter, 1874
6. Lafayette Bridge, 1968
7. Union Depot, Fourth and Sibley, 1923
8. Warner Road Park, 1994
9. State Capitol, 1905

1   2 3   4

6   7   1   2   8   9   4

Downtown

South from Merriam's Hill, 1889

This panoramic view from above the intersection of University Avenue (behind the fountain) and Robert Street (lower left) provides a marvelous look at the St. Paul skyline after the great building boom of the 1880s. Although the city had already grown its share of skyscrapers by this time, the skyline retains a rather spiky profile, with the towers of churches and public buildings still dominating the scene.

What is perhaps most striking about this image is the denseness and variety of the urban world it depicts. Buildings of all types crowd together in a way that suggests something from the old quarters of Europe (although the tall commercial buildings and simple wooden houses in view are emphatically American). The photographer was stationed near what was once known as Merriam's Overlook—a beautifully landscaped cul-de-sac at the end of Sherburne Avenue above and behind the site occupied today by the State Capitol.

In 1889 before Cass Gilbert's Capitol building appeared on the scene, the hilltop along Sherburne was occupied by a row of mansions. Among them were the homes of William Merriam, then governor of the state (he served from 1889 to 1893), and his father John Merriam, a prominent St. Paul businessman. The Merriams owned neighboring mansions on either side of Cedar Street—William's to the east and John's to the west.

The panoramic view was taken from the grounds of William Merriam's house and shows a small pond with fountain, winding paths, and a huge lawn newly planted with trees. The identity of the three young women by the pond is unknown. They clearly come from a well-to-do family (perhaps even the Merriams), since one of the girls is holding a tennis racquet. Another historic photograph, shot in about 1890 from Robert Street looking west, offers an excellent view of William Merriam's mansion and the elegant stone stairway leading up to the lookout.

Today the pond and fountain, the staircase, the overlook, the mansions, and most of the 1889 skyline are gone. The manicured lawn where the three girls once posed for their picture on a summer afternoon is now a steep, weedy hillside that climbs up from University Avenue toward a state parking lot. But there is still an overlook—a rather grim concrete affair—and the view south toward the modern St. Paul skyline remains impressive, though hardly what it was a century ago.

Buildings and Places

1. Pioneer Press (now Pioneer) Building, Fourth and Robert, 1889, 1910
2. Visitation Convent (later St. Paul Hospital), University and Robert, J. C. McCarthy, 1889–1934
3. Globe Building, Fourth and Cedar, E. Townsend Mix, 1887–1959
4. St. Paul City Hall–Ramsey County Courthouse, Fourth and Cedar, 1889–1933
5. Central Park Methodist Church, Twelfth and Minnesota, 1887–1961
6. Second State Capitol, Tenth and Wabasha, 1883–1938
7. Assumption Catholic Church, Seventh (formerly Ninth) near St. Peter, 1874
8. William Merriam House, 25 University Ave., Clarence H. Johnston, 1882–ca. 1900
9. Galtier Plaza, Sixth and Jackson, 1986
10. First National Bank (now First Bank) Building, Fourth and Minnesota, Graham, Anderson, Probst, and White, 1931
11. World Trade Center, Seventh and Wabasha, 1987
12. St. Paul Companies, Sixth and Washington, 1991
13. Minnesota Judicial Building, Cedar and Constitution, Leonard Parker Associates, 1990, 1995

Ca. 1890   8

9   10   11   12   13

Wabasha Street

North from Thirteenth Street, 1949

The rather seedy residential area that once surrounded the State Capitol was near the end of
its life when this photograph was taken. Urban
renewal on a grand scale lay just around the
corner, and hints of what was to come are clearly visible.
Numerous vacant lots, always a sign of trouble, dot the
landscape, and the old buildings at right are in an
advanced state of dilapidation. Yet there are some pleasing

images in this photograph as well. The spire of Trinity
Evangelical Lutheran Church provides a nice counterpoint
to the towering white dome of the Capitol, while the Ferris
Hotel (left) presents a handsome Edwardian street front.

Perhaps the most pleasing sight of all, however, is the
streamlined streetcar caught by the photographer just as it
passes a work crew repairing the northbound tracks on
Wabasha. Twin City Rapid Transit Company bought 141
of the new cars between 1945 and 1948 in an effort to
upgrade service and present a more modern image.
Streetcars at this time were still a vital part of the Twin
Cities mass transit system, which in 1949 attracted 165
million riders a year, fewer than in the 1920s but far higher
than the number today. But the streetcars were living on
borrowed time, and by 1954 they were gone, in part

4

because of the criminality of the transit company's owners, the notorious Kid Cann syndicate.

The old neighborhood around the Capitol disappeared at nearly the same time. By 1949 the city and state were already committed to building today's Capitol Mall, a decision that culminated many years of planning aimed at improving the Capitol's setting. Cass Gilbert, the Capitol's designer, had been the first to suggest a more dignified foreground for the building. Between 1903 and 1931, Gilbert produced at least three plans for a mall (and connecting grand boulevards), but he did not live to see his dream fulfilled. In 1945 the state legislature finally approved a mall plan, and major clearance work began five years later. By the mid-1950s, the mall was largely completed.

Today's view shows how thoroughly the mall transformed this part of St. Paul. Wabasha north of Twelfth is gone, as are most of the buildings and many of the streets seen in the old photograph. Sprinklers now water the great green lawn that covers the rubble of the past.

Buildings and Places

1. Ferris Hotel, Wabasha near Thirteenth, ca. 1910–ca. 50

2. Trinity Evangelical Lutheran Church, Wabasha and Tilton (street no longer exists), George Wirth, 1886–1952

3. Christ Lutheran Church on Capitol Hill, University and Park, Buechner and Orth, 1911

4. State Capitol, 1905

Cedar Street

Northeast from Plaza of State Capitol, 1937

Although it is actually the third building to serve as Minnesota's seat of government, the current State Capitol somehow seems immune to the hard hand of time. Like the nearby St. Paul Cathedral (the fourth of its kind), the Capitol is a rock of stability in the roiling seas of change that have washed away so much of historic St. Paul. Because the Capitol has not budged, these then-and-now photographs, which use the building's east steps as a common reference point,

make for a very precise comparison (although sharp-eyed observers may note that the drain in the foreground has been moved slightly over the years).

Yet one of the supreme ironies of the Capitol—a building associated with all that is enduring in civic life—is that it has proved to be an agent of urban destruction. Like a bright new star, the Capitol created its own gravitational pull, attracting a constellation of government buildings that gradually overwhelmed the world around it. This process of government place-making culminated in the early 1950s with the creation of the Capitol Mall.

In 1937, however, there was no big mall. Instead the Capitol presided over a defiantly déclassé neighborhood of decaying mansions, cheap apartment houses, and rundown commercial properties. This very American juxtaposition of grandeur and shabbiness grated on the civic nerves.

1   5

There were frequent calls to clear out the old neighborhood, which one newspaper described as a "screen of ugliness" blocking views of the Capitol.

A small piece of this neighborhood appears in the 1937 photograph. Across Cedar from the Capitol's east steps are a trio of weary Victorians—the Maurice Lyons mansion (by this time a boardinghouse), another dwelling, and the Hiawatha Apartments. On a nearby hill, looming over everything with a kind of dark majesty, is the George G. Benz house. One of the most romantic of all St. Paul mansions, the Benz house—built for a German immigrant who made his fortune in distilling—featured a four-story tower and a grand staircase described as "a sight never to be forgotten." The Benz house and a row of mansions around it were all swept away by the relentless expansion of state government, as were the old buildings on Cedar.

Today the view across Cedar shows a plaza created in 1990 when the old Minnesota Historical Society Building was turned into a new home for the state's judiciary. Meanwhile the hilltop along Sherburne Avenue where the Benz house once stood so proudly has become a state parking lot that provides vacant automobiles with one of the city's finest views.

Buildings and Places

1. State Capitol (east steps), 1905
2. George G. Benz house, 5 Sherburne Ave., Emil W. Ulrici, 1888–1948
3. Maurice Lyons house, 720 Cedar St., ca. 1885–1958
4. Hiawatha Apartments, 702–710 Cedar St. (at Aurora Ave.), ca. 1890s–1958
5. East Capitol plaza, adjacent to Minnesota Judicial Building (formerly Minnesota Historical Society Building), Richard Fleischner (artist), 1990

Twelfth Street

West from Jackson Street, 1945

The neighborhood south of the State Capitol once could boast of a number of mansions, but as early as the 1870s its fortunes began to decline. For much of the twentieth century the area was considered a slum, and this photograph shows why. Evidence of neglect is everywhere, from the leaning street sign to the unkempt yards to the boarded-up windows on the Market Produce Company, named for its proximity to the old city market a block away. Market Produce, incidentally, was originally built as the home of Simeon P. Folsom, who became St. Paul's first city surveyor in 1854.

Yet this scene also has undeniable appeal because it depicts the sort of mixed commercial-residential neighborhood that has all but disappeared from St. Paul (Grand Avenue being one splendid exception). The architectural ensemble here forms an open-air museum of historic styles. The steeple of Central Park Methodist Church, a Romanesque-inspired design, dominates the scene. Forming a neoclassic foil across the street (where the St. Paul Saints had a baseball park from 1903 to 1910) is the gleaming white terra-cotta façade of the Purity Baking Company. The owners of the bakery, which cost $1 million to build in 1913, claimed it was then the largest in the world, with a capacity of 140,000 loaves of bread a day. Faintly visible behind the bakery is another, much larger neoclassic monument—the St. Paul Cathedral. Other

buildings in view include a Victorian-era commercial block (to the left of the church) and Greek Revival and Italianate-style houses on the south side of Twelfth.

Except for the well-dressed man in the street, who may have been doing advance work for highway construction (envisioned in this area as early as 1945), the people here—including the toddler playing in the dirt—do not appear affluent. This was a working-class neighborhood, and like others of its kind it was soon to bear the brunt of urban renewal and freeway construction.

Today's photograph, taken from a vantage point slightly to the south of the 1945 picture, reveals that every last vestige of this old urban ensemble, except for the Cathedral, is gone. Much of it was plowed under for Interstate 94, which consumed the south side of Twelfth in the early 1960s. Central Park Methodist, razed in 1961, was among the first to fall. On the north side of Twelfth, everything has been

swallowed by the State Capitol campus. The bakery, which closed in 1991, was the longest survivor, its aroma providing one of the few pleasures of a drive through Spaghetti Junction. It was finally torn down in 1993.

Buildings and Places

1. Henry Hensel house, 140 E. Twelfth St., 1872–ca. 1960
2. Central Park Methodist Church, Twelfth and Minnesota, George Wirth, 1887–1961
3. St. Paul Cathedral, Summit and Selby, 1914
4. Purity Baking Co. (later Taystee Bakery), Twelfth between Minnesota and Robert, 1913–93
5. Lovene Apartments, Twelfth near Jackson, ca. 1890–ca. 1960
6. Market Produce Co. (originally Simeon P. Folsom house), Twelfth and Jackson, ca. 1850s–ca. 1960
7. Interstate 94, opened 1967

Fifth Street

West toward Third Street (Kellogg Boulevard), ca. 1919

St. Paulites pride themselves, with some justice, on their city's sense of history, a virtue generally thought to be lacking in more modern-minded Minneapolis. It is certainly true that large parts of St. Paul, especially in the residential neighborhoods around lower Summit Avenue, are models of historic

preservation. Yet in one important preservation category— historic streets—St. Paul has actually been far more destructive than its larger neighbor across the river.

Nowhere has St. Paul's traditional street pattern been more extensively altered than in the western part of downtown. This photograph is a heartbreaking case in point. It was taken along Fifth just east of its intersection with Third (now Kellogg Boulevard) and Pleasant Avenue (which crosses in front of the old wooden row house at left center).

The photograph is charming in every respect, beginning with the little girl standing in the car. Who the girl was or why she posed here is unknown, but she adds a wonderful human face to the architectural setting around her. Fifth at

4 2 5

this time featured a blend of houses and small commercial buildings, all set off from the street at an odd angle because blocks in this part of town tended to be wedge-shaped rather than square. Businesses in view include the St. Paul Dairy Company (its sign is in front of the badly tilting power pole at center) and a barber shop next to the girl's car. Rising above these rather humble structures are two of the city's great monuments—the St. Paul Cathedral and the Amherst Wilder mansion with its picturesque witch's-hat roof.

Today this part of Fifth and the modest but appealing neighborhood it once served are gone. The construction of Interstate 35E, decades of urban renewal that began with the massive Civic Center project in the early 1970s, plus the widening, straightening, moving, and elimination of

numerous streets all conspired to wipe out virtually every trace of the old neighborhood. Only the Cathedral remains, towering now over the vacant remnants of progress.

Buildings and Places

1. Amherst H. Wilder house, 226 Summit Ave., 1887–1959
2. St. Paul Cathedral, Selby and Summit, Emmanuel L. Masqueray, 1914
3. St. Paul Dairy Co., Fifth and Third, ca. 1880–ca. 1960s
4. Interstate 35E (behind parking lot), opened 1990
5. Catholic Education Center (formerly Cathedral School), Kellogg Blvd. and College Ave., ca. 1920

Seven Corners

Northeast on Seventh Street from Third Street (Kellogg Boulevard), ca. 1902–04

Once upon a time, there really was a Seven Corners in St. Paul. Created by colliding grids at the western edge of downtown, the original Seven Corners dates to 1849 and brought together five streets: Seventh (down which the camera is pointing),

Third (at far right), Fourth (just past the towered Defiel Block at right center), Main (at far left next to the Bromley Livery Stable), and Eagle (which came in just past the lower right corner of this photograph and is not visible).

Seven Corners was usually a busy place, but it looks awfully quiet here, which suggests that the photograph was taken on a Sunday. With their long exposure times, early photographs often produced blurred "ghosts" in the final print. But the people in this picture—the policeman in the middle of the intersection, the bicyclist on Fourth, the horsemen by the stable—are in such clear focus that they must have posed for the camera.

Dominating this scene is the Defiel Block, a wonderful

piece of Victorian street theater built by St. Paul entrepreneur Michael Defiel, who made his fortune in the ice business. The building was designed by Hermann Kretz, whose surviving works include the Commerce Building a few blocks away. Wedged between Third and Fourth, the Defiel's bell-shaped tower punctuates the intersection like a big exclamation point and was for many years a Seven Corners landmark. The ground floor housed retail shops, including a drugstore plastered with advertisements for such diverse products as Duke of Parma cigars and a brand of electric belt said to be a sure-fire cure for "nervous troubles."

Another landmark—Assumption Church—is visible here, though just barely: the tops of its twin steeples can be seen peeking out over the livery stable. The Bromley stable (for whose owner this photograph may have been taken) was one of about forty such facilities in St. Paul at the turn of the century. While electric streetcars were in widespread service at this time, horse power remained the dominant mode of transport for delivery vehicles and for those wealthy enough to own a carriage. Naturally all of this horse traffic produced horse manure, piles of which can be seen scattered along the streets.

Four other historic photographs provide a look at Seven Corners from a variety of angles, including a 1933 view from northwest toward Third. Seventh is at lower right,

10　　2　　　　11　　　　12

Fourth at lower left. Note how the streetcar tracks coming from Fourth—the Selby Avenue line—curve across the intersection toward Third. Also note the single track that turns sharply from Seventh onto Main, where a truck awaits its chance to get through the intersection. Buildings visible here include the Moore Block (at left); built in 1871 it once contained the offices of many members of the medical profession. Behind and to the right of the Moore Block is the many-chimneyed Summit Avenue mansion of James J. Hill.

A 1932 photograph shows Seven Corners as it looked from about a block to the east on Third. The St. Paul Cathedral, as it does from so many places in the city, towers over the scene. The old limestone building at left is the Irvine Block, also known as the Flatiron Building and Forty Lights Hotel (a reference to its numerous windows). Many of those lights were undoubtedly red at one time, since Seven Corners was something of a tenderloin district in the late nineteenth century. Both the Irvine and Defiel blocks fell to the wrecker in 1936 when Third was widened to become Kellogg Boulevard. A 1935 photograph looking east down Third from Seven Corners shows just how narrow the old street was before construction.

Yet another view, from nearly the same vantage point as the turn-of-the-century picture, reveals how much change had already occurred at Seven Corners by 1956. The Defiel Block has been replaced, rather ignominiously, by a Roto-Rooter outlet, and many other historic buildings are gone. However, Fabel's Shoes (founded in 1856 and destined to remain in business until 1981) still holds down one corner. Seventh has also been widened, while the wall of buildings that once defined the intersection has been breached by parking lots and other modern intrusions.

1933   5   6   1

Today Seven Corners—dominated by the dreary hulk of the St. Paul Civic Center arena—has lost much of its historic character. It has also lost two streets—Fourth and Main. Both were amputated from the intersection when the arena was built in the early 1970s. Construction of the arena also required the realignment of both Kellogg and Seventh, so that the 1995 view (looking along the old line of Seventh) appears to be at a different angle from the 1902–04 view.

The unhappy result of these changes is that Seven Corners now has the open, ill-defined look of a suburban crossroads. Fortunately a row of old buildings remains along Seventh Street west of the intersection, forming a pleasant little commercial enclave. The success of this old shopping district suggests how all of Seven Corners might have evolved had the city taken more care to preserve its historic character.

1932   **7**   **8** **5** **9**

Buildings and Places

1. W. H. Bromley Livery Stable (later an auto garage), Seventh and Main, ca. 1880, ca. 1930s–ca. 70
2. Assumption Catholic Church (only tips of steeples visible in 1902 photograph), Seventh (formerly Ninth) near St. Peter, Eduard Reidel, 1874
3. Arlington Hotel, between Fourth and Seventh, ca. 1870s–ca. 1936
4. Defiel Block, between Third and Fourth at Seventh, Hermann Kretz & Co., 1889–1936
5. Moore Block, Third and Seventh, 1871–1974
6. James J. Hill house, 240 Summit Ave., 1891
7. Irvine Block (Many Lights Hotel), Third and Eagle, ca. 1854–1936
8. Forepaugh Block, Third and Seventh, 1883, ca. 1930s
9. St. Paul Cathedral, Selby and Summit, 1914
10. The Pointe Apartments, Tenth and Minnesota, Miller Hanson, Westerbeck, and Bell, 1988
11. World Trade Center, Seventh and Wabasha, 1987
12. St. Paul Civic Center arena (site of Defiel Block), Seventh and Kellogg, Convention Center Architects and Engineers, 1973

1935   **4**   **7**

1956   **1**   **8**

Main Street

North from Seven Corners, 1906

St. Paul has always been a bit odd when it comes to street names, and Main is no exception. Main, which acquired its misleading name in the same year this photograph was taken (before then it was called Fort), was never anything like a major thoroughfare. In fact it runs for just four blocks on the western margin of downtown. Yet it was once quite nice in its own way, bearing no resemblance to the ragged remnant of a street it has become.

The 1906 photograph shows virtually the entire extent of Main, which ran due north from Seventh (at Seven Cor-ners) past Fifth, Sixth, and Ninth (in that classically in-comprehensible St. Paul order) before ending at Tenth. At the turn of the century, it was a typical edge-of-downtown street, which is to say that it accommodated a jumble of uses—residential, institutional, commercial, and industrial.

The residential is represented by several houses, including five apparently identical wood-frame dwellings tucked behind the Bromley Livery Stable at right. The Bucking-ham Apartments, as they were known at this time, can also be seen at far left. Institutional structures in view include the recently completed State Capitol and, to its right, the towered mass of Cretin High School at Sixth and Main. Bromley's stable and several small shops across from it provide a modest commercial presence. The largest manufacturer in view is Mitsch and Heck Company at Fifth and Main. The firm—formed in 1892 by two German immigrants, Mathias Heck and Lorenz Mitsch—made wagons and later automobiles. Over the years, Main and its old

buildings gradually adapted to new uses, with automobile garages becoming especially common by the 1920s.

Today all of the nineteenth-century buildings once found on and around Main are gone except for the Armstrong-Quinlan house, a vacant and deteriorating monument from 1886. Meanwhile Main itself has evolved toward the point of invisibility, as a contemporary view from Seven Corners illustrates. Half of the street, the segment from Seventh to Sixth, has been swallowed up by the city's insatiable appetite for traffic improvement and street realignment at Seven Corners (see page 152). What remains of poor old Main is a two-block stretch between Sixth and Tenth sandwiched between freeways, access ramps, and parking lots. The modern era, in short, has made Main an even more inaptly named street than it was in 1906. Incidentally the fellow standing by the stoplight in the foreground and no doubt brooding upon the sorry state of progress is the author.

Buildings and Places

1. Buckingham Apartments (originally Hotel Barteau, later Piedmont Apartments), Ninth and Smith, 1889–1969
2. State Capitol, 1905
3. Trinity Evangelical Lutheran Church, Wabasha and Tilton, 1886–1952
4. Cretin High School, Sixth and Main, 1889–ca. 1925
5. Mitsch & Heck Co., Fifth and Main, 1892–ca. 1970
6. W. H. Bromley Livery Stable, Seventh and Main, ca. 1880, ca. 1930s–ca. 70
7. St. Paul Armory (roof only visible), Sixth and Exchange, Hermann Kretz, 1904–63
8. Armstrong-Quinlan house, Fifth St. near Kellogg Blvd., Edward P. Bassford, 1886
9. Labor and Professional Centre, Sixth and Main, 1976
10. Catholic Charities building (site of Cretin High School), Sixth and Main, ca. 1925

Pleasant Avenue

West from near Kellogg Boulevard, ca. 1940

It does not require an especially fine sense of irony to see how these two photographs demonstrate the transforming power of the automobile. An avenue that in 1940 was devoted to selling automobiles and related merchandise has today succumbed to its own success, every last vestige of its existence having been wiped out by a freeway. It might be called poetic justice, although the urbanistic consequences of Pleasant Avenue's destruction are hardly the stuff of poetry.

The 1940 view shows how extensively the automobile business had come to dominate the western part of downtown St. Paul by that time. Several dealerships (for Buick, Chrysler, and Packard, among others) are visible, as are such auto-related businesses as a tire store and a D-X service station.

Tucked beneath the commanding bluff of Summit Avenue, this stretch of Pleasant was mostly residential in the nineteenth century. Visible behind and to the right of the Chrysler sign is a survivor from that era, the splendid old Oakhurst Apartments, which originally featured eight-room suites with wrought-iron balconies. But the avenue's

major monument was the People's Church, once the largest Protestant congregation in the city. Its huge auditorium, with seating for thirty-five hundred, attracted many notable speakers, including Mark Twain and Winston Churchill. Vacated in 1939 when the congregation disbanded, the building was destroyed by fire a year later, not long after this photograph was taken.

Another historic photograph, taken in 1952, provides a view of Pleasant in the opposite direction, looking east from Kellogg. Old rooming houses and apartments crowd along the south side of the street, across from the Buick dealership. The big turreted building in the center is one of St. Paul's grand Victorians—the Piedmont Apartments at Ninth Street and Smith Avenue.

Beginning in the late 1960s, most of the buildings in these photographs were cleared away for Interstate 35E. Much of Pleasant vanished with them. Legal battles delayed construction of the freeway for twenty years, however, and it was only in 1990 that the road finally opened all the way to Interstate 94. As part of the freeway work, Kellogg Boulevard was moved a block east of its 1940 intersection with Pleasant. Because of these changes and the absence of old landmarks, the new picture represents at best an educated guess as to the spot where the photographer stood in 1940 to record what is now a vanished piece of St. Paul.

5   6   *1952*

1   2   3   4   5

7   8   9

Downtown and Capitol Hill

Northeast from Summit and Dayton Avenues, 1890

Like many a Victorian tycoon in St. Paul, Norman W. Kittson built an enormous house on Summit Avenue that offered just about everything except comfort and good taste. It also failed to confer immortality, since Kittson—who made his fortune in steamboats, railroads, and real estate—died only four years after the mansion's completion in 1884. Nonetheless his short-lived dream house proved to be of considerable benefit to history because its unusually tall tower was an ideal place for taking panoramic photographs of St. Paul.

One such picture offers a superb look at the burgeoning city. The camera is pointed down Summit toward today's State Capitol area. Summit Park, a green triangle created in the 1880s, is on the left. All around are stately dwellings, among them the Arnold Kalman mansion with its picturesque carriage house. An intriguing feature of this photograph is the light mast rising above the intersection of Summit, Dayton, and Third Street. Masts such as this, designed to illuminate a wide area with arc lights, were

9   10   11

erected in many cities in the 1880s but worked so poorly that most were gone within a decade. This mast was one of two in St. Paul (the other was at Third and Wabasha).

Another view from Kittson's tower, this one taken toward the southeast in 1903, shows the beautifully landscaped grounds of the Amherst Wilder estate. It also provides a rare glimpse of the counterweighted cable-car system installed in 1898 on the Selby Avenue hill, which was too steep for standard electric streetcars to negotiate. The system used small helper cars (two are visible here) that gripped moving cables under the tracks, giving an extra push to streetcars going up the hill and providing better braking for those going down. This cumbersome system was replaced in 1907 by the Selby Avenue tunnel, which cut the grade to 7 percent and thus made normal streetcar operation possible.

Kittson's mansion came down in 1905, and the new view was taken from its replacement, the St. Paul Cathedral. Shot from a dormer near the Cathedral's north bell tower, the picture reveals that almost everything from the 1890 photograph is gone. Old buildings have been razed and new ones built, streets (including part of

Summit) have been moved, and even Summit Park has been reconfigured. Still two blocks of old Summit and a part of old Third remain, like lines from a drawing whose image has otherwise faded away.

1903   6   7   8

Downtown

East from Sixth Street and Summit Avenue, ca. 1916

This wonderful view of the downtown skyline and the old College Avenue residential district was taken from the Marlborough Apartments, a six-story building that once stood at the southeast corner of Sixth and Summit. What makes the photograph so fascinating is that it shows how heavily built-up the neighborhood beneath lower Summit Avenue was at one time.

College Avenue, which originally extended all the way from Third Street (Kellogg Boulevard) to Cedar Street on a course parallel to Summit, was still largely residential in 1916. Among the dwellings visible here is St. Paul's only

octagon house, built in the 1850s for pioneer banker and real estate agent George W. Farrington. Octagon houses were a minor fad in the mid-nineteenth century. However, they proved to be so terribly inefficient that only a few thousand were ever built in the United States. In the lower right-hand corner is another landmark—the old Morris Lamprey house at 137 West College. This Italianate-style stone mansion was for many years home to the Capital City Hebrew Congregation and School.

The downtown buildings in this scene include several familiar monuments, such as Central Presbyterian Church, Assumption Catholic Church, and the old Federal Courts Building (Landmark Center). Note also the steel framework to the right of Assumption's twin towers. This is the Hamm Building, which was begun as a new home for the Mannheimer Brothers Department Store. But financial problems halted construction in 1915, and only a bare steel skeleton stood until 1919, when brewer William Hamm finally completed the project as an office building.

1 2 3 4 5 6 7 8 9

10   11   12

The Marlborough Apartments came down in 1972, and today's view was taken from the roof of the Minnesota History Center, whose grassy courtyard occupies the site of the apartment building. The view shows how completely this part of St. Paul has changed since 1916. College Avenue itself is all but gone (only a one-block stretch west of Kellogg Boulevard survives), and the old houses and apartments have vanished as well.

A number of these historic structures (including Farrington's house) were cleared out as early as 1920 to make way for Miller Hospital, which in turn was demolished for the History Center in the late 1980s. But it was the construction of Interstates 94 and 35E, beginning in the 1960s, that wiped out much of the old College Avenue neighborhood. Not surprisingly, the downtown skyline has also been transformed in the years since 1916, with modern office buildings now towering over the old church steeples that were so prominent eighty years ago.

Buildings and Places

1. Colonnade (Willard) Apartments, Tenth and St. Peter, 1889 (Allen H. Stem), 1899, 1955, ca. 1980s
2. Second State Capitol, Tenth and Wabasha, 1883–1938
3. Central Presbyterian Church, Cedar and Exchange, 1889
4. George W. Farrington house, 125 W. College, 1857–ca. 1920
5. Assumption Catholic Church, Seventh (formerly Ninth) near St. Peter, 1874
6. Hamm Building (structural frame only visible in ca. 1916 view), Sixth and St. Peter, 1920
7. Morris Lamprey house, 137 W. College, 1871–1944
8. Federal Courts Building (Landmark Center), Fifth between Market and Washington, 1892, 1902
9. Buckingham Apartments (originally Hotel Barteau, later Piedmont Apartments), Ninth and Smith, 1889–1969
10. Minnesota History Center, Kellogg and John Ireland, 1992
11. World Trade Center, Seventh and Wabasha, 1987
12. St. Paul Companies, Sixth and Washington, 1991

Downtown

Northeast from Smith Avenue High Bridge, ca. 1912

Of all the urban vistas in the Twin Cities, none matches the view east from the Smith Avenue High Bridge. The great sweep of the river, the bluffs rising from the wide glacial valley, and the profile of the downtown skyline all combine to create a memorable visual experience. It is hardly a surprise, therefore, that the upper end of the High Bridge at Cherokee Heights on the West Side has long been a favorite spot for photographers.

The 1912 view is of interest on several counts. For one, it provides an excellent view of downtown St. Paul at a time when the sixteen-story Pioneer Building still retained its top-of-the-skyline bragging rights. This picture also shows the scene of a spectacular disaster that had occurred just a few years earlier. It happened on August 20, 1904, when a tornado packing winds of 180 miles an hour delivered a ferocious hit to the High Bridge and sent its five southernmost spans (the bridge had twenty-four spans in all) plunging into the Mississippi. The bridge did not reopen until June 1905.

Besides showing off a piece of the only Twin Cities bridge ever assaulted by a twister, the old photograph offers views of the downtown skyline, the old Upper Levee Flats (see page 184), and Harriet Island when it was indeed a real island. Several structures on the island are visible

1　　　　**2**　　**3**　**4**　　　**5**　　**6** **7** **8 9**　　　**10**

| 1 | 2 | 4 11 | 5 | 12 | 7 |

here, among them a large stilted pavilion near the western end. The pavilion, like other buildings on the park, was raised off the ground to withstand the floods that periodically inundated the island. Named after pioneer teacher Harriet Bishop, the island park was dedicated in 1905 and once included a small zoo, an amusement park, and public beaches. The beach, however, was closed in about 1922 when water tests confirmed what most people already knew—the Mississippi in this part of St. Paul had become an open sewer.

The 1995 photograph shows that almost everything is different from the way it was in 1912. The old High Bridge has been replaced, Harriet Island is no longer an island (its back channel was filled in around 1950), and modern skyscrapers now dominate the skyline. A few enduring architectural symbols remain, of course, such as the State Capitol, Landmark Center, and Assumption Catholic Church. But the one truly timeless element in these photographs is the Mississippi Valley, still the grandest place in St. Paul.

Buildings and Places

1. State Capitol, 1905
2. Assumption Catholic Church, Seventh (formerly Ninth) near St. Peter, 1874
3. Smith Avenue High Bridge, Keystone Bridge Co. and others, 1889–1985; new bridge, Strgar-Roscoe-Fausch, Inc., and others, 1987
4. Federal Courts Building (Landmark Center), Fifth between Market and Washington, 1892, 1902
5. St. Paul Hotel, Fifth and St. Peter, 1910, 1981, 1990
6. Lowry Medical Arts Building, St. Peter between Fourth and Fifth, Kees and Colburn, 1912
7. Harriet Island Park, developed 1905
8. St. Paul City Hall–Ramsey County Courthouse, Fourth and Cedar, 1889–1933
9. Commerce Building, Fourth and Wabasha, Hermann Kretz, 1910
10. Pioneer Building, Fourth and Robert, 1889, 1910
11. World Trade Center, Seventh and Wabasha, 1987
12. First Bank (originally First National Bank) Building, Fourth and Minnesota, 1931

St. Paul
Neighborhoods

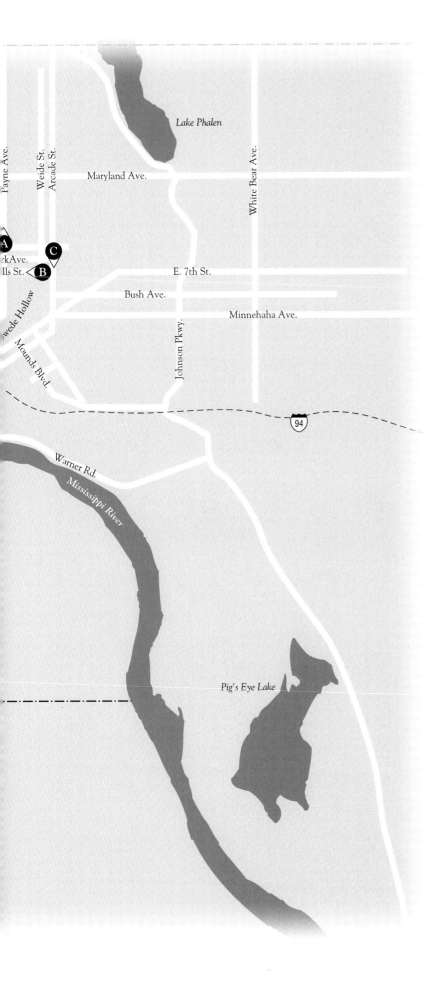

St. Paul
Neighborhoods

A. Payne Avenue

B. Wells Street

C. Arcade Street

D. University Avenue, toward Rice and Wabasha Streets

E. University Avenue, from Snelling Avenue

F. Raymond Avenue

G. Selby Avenue

H. Upper Levee Flats ("Little Italy")

I. West Side Flats

J. Wabasha Street, from Fillmore Avenue

This street map was drawn from a 1934 map of St. Paul.

Payne Avenue

North from Case Avenue, ca. 1905

Payne Avenue was for many years St. Paul's Swedish street. Immigrants from that country had settled in nearby Swede Hollow by 1850, and as their fortunes improved, many moved up (literally) to the Payne Avenue area. Originally commercial development concentrated along the lower part of the avenue, but the completion of a bridge across the railroad tracks near Bush Avenue in 1893 quickly fueled expansion to the north. Most of Payne, however, was never served by a streetcar line. Despite this seeming drawback, Payne has remained the main shopping street of St. Paul's Lower East Side for more than a century.

This atmospheric photograph presents an early image of the avenue in all of its rough glory. In 1905 Payne still had the look of a frontier street, unpaved and a bit untamed, its commercial life conducted from simple brick and wooden storefronts, almost all of which were built by Swedish immigrants. A number of these establishments—such as F. J. Tripanier's pool hall at right and, a bit farther down the street, Adolph's Tavern—served the working men of the neighborhood.

The vitality of the avenue is abundantly evident. Delivery wagons, including one with a huge load of hay

1

2

and another (in front of Adolph's) carrying barrels of Pabst Beer, can be seen all along the avenue. Everybody else, however, seems to be on foot (note how many people are walking up the hill), for this was not the sort of street where one was likely to see a lot of swells in carriages. There are also plenty of youngsters about, dressed against the chill and obviously not concerned in the least about standing in the middle of the street to pose for posterity.

Today the look of the avenue has changed a bit, with new buildings added here and there and the old ones sporting updated façades. And as with many commercial streets in the inner-city portions of St. Paul and Minneapolis, Payne has had to battle for business against suburban malls and all the other dispersing forces of the modern retail market. Yet the old avenue has done all right, and its essential character has changed little since the turn of the century. It is still not upscale, and it is still a street where working-class folks from the neighborhood come to shop, eat, and maybe hoist a few brews at their favorite tavern. One hopes it will ever be so.

Buildings and Places

1. Wood-frame store building, Payne and Case, 1888–ca. 1922
2. Tripanier's pool hall (later Jackson, Lyceum Theaters), Payne near Case, ca. 1880–1976
3. Commercial building (originally First State Bank), Payne and Case, 1923

3

Wells Street

West from near Weide Street, ca. 1900

St. Paul's Lower East Side is like no other neighborhood in the Twin Cities. Cut by deep ravines filled with railroad tracks and built on a series of steep hills, the neighborhood in places looks astonishingly eastern, like a small piece of Pennsylvania somehow transported to the Midwest. The area's numerous historic houses (including several of the oldest in St. Paul) and often narrow streets add to its distinctive flavor.

One of the neighborhood's most fascinating streets is Wells, seen here just east of Payne Avenue. Graded along the side of a precipitous hill that comes up from the northern end of Swede Hollow, Wells is a genuine rarity in the Twin Cities: a split street, with the upper and lower sections separated by a massive stone wall. The battered limestone wall, a beautiful example of the mason's art, dates from 1892. It was probably built as the cheapest solution to a difficult problem: the houses on the left are so far below those atop the hill to the right that only a two-level street could serve both. Without the wall, two separate streets might well have been required.

The photograph also shows how ragged this part of St. Paul was in 1900. The sidewalks are wooden planks, the streets are muddy channels, trees are in short supply,

2

4

and few property owners appear infatuated with the idea of a perfectly sodded yard. Much of St. Paul looked like this at the turn of the century and thus bore little resemblance to the far more frequently photographed Summit Avenue. The realities of life before the advent of indoor plumbing are also evident here: note the privy behind the hilltop house at right center.

Today although the scenery has changed a bit, Wells retains its unusual two-tiered character. The wall is showing its age and has lost its original iron-pipe railing, but it is surviving the battle against the forces of gravity. Houses, including at least one (at far left) visible in the old photograph, continue to line the south side of the street, their backyards overlooking the railroad tracks that still follow the ravine below. This scene may not last, however,

because in 1995 the city began considering plans to build a new road and industrial park in the railroad corridor south of Wells. On the north side, change came many years ago when the old Johnson High School replaced some of the houses.

Buildings and Places

1. Ravine north of Swede Hollow (behind houses at left)
2. Payne Ave. (past end of wall)
3. House, Wells at Weide St., ca. 1880
4. St. Paul Public Schools building (originally Johnson High School), York Ave. at Weide, 1911

Arcade Street

South from York Avenue, 1944

A significant piece of St. Paul's industrial history—and a longtime East Side institution—appears in this photograph from the World War II era. The large complex of buildings on the left is the Seeger Refrigerator Company, which at its height manufactured 10 percent of the nation's refrigerators (many of them sold by Sears, Roebuck) and employed more than five thousand people. Among the company's most famous products was the Cold Spot Super 6. Introduced in 1935, it was the first refrigerator to come with the sleek, streamlined look later used for many other home appliances.

Seeger expanded the Arcade Street plant frequently over the years, and it had grown to nearly 650,000 square feet (occupying more than fourteen acres) by the time of this photograph. Like virtually every other American manufacturer, Seeger churned out military products during the war years, including bomb racks for B-29 bombers. With gasoline in short supply, the bulk of the plant's wartime workforce arrived by streetcar, one of which can be seen heading north on Arcade. Lana Turner is also part of the picture. Looking suitably vampish, she adorns the billboard at far left, posed for her latest movie, a now forgotten MGM epic entitled *Marriage Is a Private Affair*.

The rest of the scene shows an urban world that had not changed much since the turn of the century: brick

streets, old-fashioned lampposts, modest houses and apartments, and a small restaurant with the inevitable Coca-Cola sign mounted on one wall. This was, one senses, a close-knit, working-class neighborhood where the rhythms of daily life maintained a comfortable stability.

This part of Arcade Street, like so many streets in old cities across America, eventually lost much of its manufacturing might. Seeger, which became a subsidiary of the Whirlpool Corporation in the 1950s, continued to prosper into the 1970s, but the old plant gradually lost its place in a harsh new landscape of worldwide competition. It closed on December 28, 1984, producing one last batch of the freezers that had become its final product.

Today the old plant and many of the houses that once surrounded it have given way to a strip mall—Seeger Square—while Arcade has been widened to accommodate increased automobile traffic. The new mall, it is said, has done quite well. But it remains to be seen whether America's transition from a manufacturing to a service economy, so starkly visible here, will prove to be as successful in the long run.

Buildings and Places

1. Seeger (later Whirlpool) Co. plant, Arcade near Wells, 1888, later additions–1984
2. Sacred Heart Catholic Church, Sixth and Arcade, ca. 1882–1946; new church, 1951
3. 3M Co. plant, Bush Ave. and E. Seventh St., Albert Kahn and Associates, 1941
4. Seeger Square shopping mall, Arcade and Wells, 1987, 1989

3   4   4

University Avenue

East toward Rice and Wabasha Streets, ca. 1916

Were it not for the dome of the State Capitol looming over everything like some august Edwardian gentleman, the location of this photograph might be quite deceptive to modern eyes. The taut arrangement of buildings and the narrow, angled streets all suggest a slice of Boston or some other East Coast city. In fact, much of St. Paul, especially the areas near downtown, once enjoyed these qualities, which may explain why visitors frequently compared the city to those in the East.

The building at the center of the photograph is the Ryan Block, a handsome Victorian from around 1890. With its corner prow, the building resembles a big ship at anchor, and one almost expects to see a captain in the tower, commanding the intersection. There were, however, no nautical enterprises in the building. Instead, its most prominent occupants, judging by sign size, were the Sylvester Brand Coal Company and a dentist named O. E. Chappell. Across University from the Ryan Block is the Ford Building, occupied in 1916 by the W. C. Schmelzel Company, an early automobile dealership. It is now used for state offices.

Another architectural gem is the mansard-roofed Florence Block, built about 1880 in the French Second Empire style. Like many buildings of its period, the Florence mixed stores on the ground floor with apartments above, some of which featured wrought-iron balconies on the second and third floors.

6   2   4

The Rice and University neighborhood appears to have been bustling at this time, and a crowd of well-dressed women can be seen standing at right, presumably waiting for a streetcar. In 1890, the first interurban streetcar line in the Twin Cities was completed along University Avenue, which remains a busy bus route to this day. Note also the policeman stationed in the intersection. He uses a hand-operated sign to direct traffic—a task that was soon to be eliminated by the introduction of signal lights.

Today's photograph shows a much-broadened intersection that has lost virtually all of its old character. The Ryan and Florence Blocks came down in 1932 when University was widened and the State Office Building was constructed just to the south. Beginning in about 1950, creation of the State Capitol Mall brought further changes to the area. The portion of Wabasha Street that once connected to Rice and University is also gone, and small nondescript buildings (one a check-cashing business) occupy two corners of the intersection. However, a new building for the Minnesota League of Cities now stands at the northwest corner of Rice and University. Featuring a small corner tower intended to evoke memories of its Victorian-era predecessors, the building has helped restore some architectural presence to the intersection.

Buildings and Places

1. Capitol Drug Co. building, Rice and University, ca. 1910–ca. 90
2. W. H. Schmelzel Co. (Ford Building), University near Park, Kees and Colburn, 1913
3. Ryan Block, Wabasha and University, ca. 1890–1932
4. State Capitol, 1905
5. Florence Block, Rice, Wabasha, and University, ca. 1880–1932
6. Minnesota League of Cities Building (site of Capitol Drug Co.), Rice and University, 1995

University Avenue

East from near Snelling Avenue, ca. 1925

These sweeping views of University Avenue in St. Paul's Midway district were taken seventy years apart from the same location—atop the three-story Ashton Building at 1549 University just east of Snelling.

The 1925 photograph shows the avenue when streetcars still ruled the road and the Montgomery Ward Company was still a giant of the American mail-order industry. The Ward's retail store and catalog warehouse on University was only four years old in 1925 but was already in the process of receiving an addition that would bring its total area under roof to 1.2 million square feet, or about twenty-seven acres. This made it the largest building in St. Paul and possibly in the Twin Cities. With its 257-foot-high water tower—said to be the tallest reinforced concrete structure in the world—the building became an instant landmark, the original monster of the Midway.

The University Avenue building was the fourth in a series of huge distribution centers built by Montgomery Ward around this time to speed delivery to its far-flung customers. During the 1920s, as many as twenty-five hundred employees worked in the building and filled up to twenty-five thousand orders a day for Ward's catalog customers throughout the Upper Midwest.

Just east of Ward's was the home of the Brown and Bigelow Company, a maker of calendars and other products. The company's plant, like the Ward's complex,

1   2   3   4   5

was set amid large, well-tended grounds—an arrangement continued today in many a suburban office park and corporate campus.

Also visible is a corner of the Snelling Avenue shops opened in 1907 by the Twin City Rapid Transit Company. The forty-acre site included a garage, substation, and shops—at least ten buildings in all by 1925. Streetcars were maintained here, and hundreds were also built through 1927.

The 1995 photograph marks the end of an era. It was taken about two months before the last remnants of the Ward's building, including the tower, were imploded on January 7, 1996. The tower and its surrounding structure were destroyed to make way for the second phase of a shopping center that includes a new Ward's store. Ward's old neighbors were also largely gone by 1995. Most of the Brown and Bigelow plant came down in 1980 and was later replaced by a motel and a Target store. A 1960s-vintage shopping center occupies most of the old streetcar property, although a large bus garage remains on the site.

Buildings and Places

1. State Capitol, 1905
2. St. Paul Casket Co. (now Music and Book Landfill, Inc.), University at Griggs St., Allen H. Stem, 1922
3. Brown & Bigelow Co., University and Syndicate St., Kees and Colburn, 1913, 1925–80 (except for auxiliary structure now known as Bigelow Building)
4. Montgomery Ward and Co. catalog house and retail store, 1400 University, Lockwood, Green & Co., 1921–96
5. Twin City Rapid Transit Co. Snelling Avenue shops, Snelling and University, 1907–ca. 60

Raymond Avenue

North from Bayless Avenue, ca. 1905

The St. Anthony Park neighborhood, with its winding streets and small parks, has always had the feel of a place apart, a sylvan village hidden away from the bustling city. This view from the turn of the century, showing a modest commercial strip along Raymond a few blocks north of University Avenue, nicely conveys the neighborhood's small-town quality.

The shops along the east side of Raymond, many sporting wooden false fronts, do indeed seem to come from some sleepy little village, although the irregular street pattern suggests a hamlet in the East rather than one in the gridironed Midwest. The most prominent business appears to be Olson and Company Hardware (right center), and it is probably safe to assume that the fellow standing in front is the store's proud proprietor. Next door is a barber shop, and farther up the street are a pharmacy, a dry goods store, and other businesses.

Across from this small commercial strip is Hampden Park, already well planted with trees. Behind the park, at the intersection of Raymond and Hampden Avenues, is a St. Paul fire station. Built in 1894, this station housed

1   2   3

1 2 3

Engine Company No. 13, which advertises its identity with a large sign. But while the city had already extended fire service to St. Anthony Park by this time, it had not yet paved the streets, a deficiency that would plague many St. Paul neighborhoods for years to come.

Today most of the small buildings seen in the 1905 view are gone. Railroad lines that came through the area in 1885 attracted industrial development, especially south of the tracks near University. Manufacturing plants, warehouses, and trucking garages have filled in the area along Hampden east of Raymond. The curving streets to the west, however, have maintained their residential character.

Despite many urban alterations, the architectural history of this small piece of St. Paul has by no means vanished. The park remains a pleasant oasis of greenery, the old fire station still stands (although it has been converted into a residence), and the handsome brick building at the southeast corner of Raymond and Hampden continues to house neighborhood businesses, including the Parkview Cafe and the Hampden Park Co-op. A small antiques store also contributes to the genteel ambiance of the avenue, which has adjusted to new urban realities without sacrificing all visible links to its past.

Buildings and Places

1. St. Paul Fire Station No. 13, Raymond and Hampden, 1894, ca. 1980
2. Hampden Park, 1885
3. Commercial building and hall, Raymond and Hampden, 1902

Selby Avenue
West from Dale Street, 1959

The intersection of Selby and Dale, despite its rich urban history, remains best known for a tragic and transforming event that occurred on August 30, 1968. On that night, the worst racial disturbance in the city's history—stemming from an incident during a dance at the St. Paul Auditorium—erupted around the intersection. Although hardly a major riot by the standards of Detroit or Los Angeles, the disturbance sparked eleven arson fires, left fifty-two people (including twenty police officers) injured, and resulted in twenty-six arrests. And, justly or not, it also left the area around Selby and Dale with a stigma that has yet to be erased.

A 1959 view shows how this section of Selby looked a decade or so before its night of troubles. It was an unprepossessing street, but it offered a decent array of shops, several small cafés, and more than a few taverns and liquor stores. There was even an old neighborhood theater (the Dale), which had shown its last movie not long before this photograph was taken.

By the early 1960s, however, the Selby–Dale area was already showing signs of blight. A variety of factors contributed to its decline, including the construction nearby of Interstate 94, which destroyed historic Rondo Avenue and caused enormous disruption to St. Paul's traditionally cohesive black community. The riot in 1968 further weakened Selby, leaving numerous boarded-up storefronts in its wake. A view from 1975 highlights the avenue's deterioration—buildings have been torn down, businesses have left, and taverns appear to be the dominant form of enterprise. Selby at this time was obviously an avenue in need of regeneration.

The view today west from Dale offers a mixed picture of failures and successes. Business and community leaders have worked hard to revitalize Selby, and significant improvements have been made, such as the cooperative apartments at right and a number of residential renovation projects. But while the nearby Selby–Western intersection saw a splurge of upscale development in the 1980s, the area west of Dale (traditionally viewed as the black section of Selby) has not come back so readily. Two of the four corners at Selby and Dale remained vacant as of 1995, although a development project was in the works. Even so, it is unlikely that Selby will ever again look as it did in 1959.

1975

1

2

Upper Levee Flats ("Little Italy")

North from Smith Avenue High Bridge, 1952

Down by the riverside has never been a trendy place to be in St. Paul because much of the city's Mississippi River shoreline is in the form of "flats" subject to frequent flooding. As a result, St. Paul's riverfront, especially in the downtown area, was largely consigned to railroad and industrial uses in the nineteenth century or became the site of squatter housing.

The Upper Levee Flats below the High Bridge developed early on as a home for some of the city's poorest residents. A variety of ethnic groups—including Poles, Bohemians, and Swedes—initially occupied the flats, living in shanties. Occasionally sheriff's deputies would roust out some of the occupants at the behest of landowners, thereby drawing the attention of the press.

In 1889 a reporter for the *St. Paul Daily Globe* observed one such eviction, but showed little sympathy for the displaced immigrants, blaming their poverty on an "insatiable thirst for beer." The reporter described a makeshift tavern on the flats as "a dark, dingy, quarrelsome den of iniquity, where the flat topers load up with the poisonous malt juice and quarrel, cut, slash, shoot and murder." One suspects this account is overly picturesque, but the fact remains that the flats cannot have been a pleasant place to live.

After 1900, however, the flats took on a different character as Italians, many of whom had come from two small towns in southern Italy, settled there in growing numbers.

Buildings and Places

1. State Capitol, 1905
2. Assumption Catholic Church, Seventh (formerly Ninth) near St. Peter, 1874
3. Farmers' Union (later Harvest States) grain elevator, Shepard Rd. near Chestnut St., 1916 (Max Toltz), 1930, 1958–89
4. Shepard Road, ca. 1960 (to be moved inland ca. 1998)

In time, the flats became a true community—poor, to be sure, but still remembered with great fondness by former residents. The 1952 photograph, taken several months after a record flood that temporarily left thousands homeless, shows how substantial a community "Little Italy" had become, even though its streets remained dirt. The houses, many with additions, are small but generally well kept, and

most have tidy backyards. Some residents made ingenious use of "found" materials in their self-built houses. For example, the Daniel Delmont house (visible here and later moved to Irvine Park) incorporated old fruit crates and driftwood into its structure.

The damage and dislocation caused by the flood convinced the city that "Little Italy" had to be removed.

Clearance began in earnest in the late 1950s, and by June 1960 the last house on the flats was gone. After completing Shepard Road through the area, the city—in a transaction not remarkable for its foresight—turned over part of the land to a scrap dealer. The junkyard was finally cleared out about 1990, and today the site stands vacant, awaiting new riverfront development.

West Side Flats

North across Wabasha Street from Prescott Point, ca. 1921

Wabasha Street

South from near Fillmore Avenue, 1954

The bluff at Prescott Point (near Hall Avenue and Prospect Boulevard) forms a promontory offering superb views of the West Side Flats and downtown skyline. A staircase and viewing platform were constructed here in the 1890s, providing an ideal place for taking panoramic pictures along Wabasha Street. The numerous photographs that resulted over the years form one of the finest then-and-now sequences available in the Twin Cities, documenting the evolution of the West Side Flats.

The flats, originally part of the Dakota County community of West St. Paul, began to attract settlers after the opening of the first Wabasha Street Bridge in 1859. But it was not until 1874 that the area was annexed to the city. Low and flood prone, the flats were one of St. Paul's poorer neighborhoods, populated by successive waves of immigrants. Many of the flats' small, flimsy houses had no sewer service or running water, causing a city planner in 1917 to call the area "a slum of the worst character." The annual spring floods were a terrible problem and produced an oddity: sand and debris deposited by the overflowing water gradually raised the overall level of the flats, so that some houses ended up fifteen feet below the street.

As time went on, the flats became increasingly industrial, especially after the construction of a levee and a railroad bridge across the river in 1885. A substantial commercial strip also developed along Wabasha, which was served by horsecar and later streetcar lines. Even so, some housing survived well into the 1950s, especially east of Robert Street.

3   9   1 10   6

1   2   *Ca. 1885*

The earliest panoramic view here, looking northeast across Wabasha Street and the flats, was taken in 1885 from a point just west of the lookout. The photograph shows work under way on the railroad swing bridge near Robert Street, where a new vehicular bridge also opened only a year later. The flats during this era were mostly residential, although a dozen or so brick commercial blocks had already sprouted along Wabasha.

A 1921 panorama from Prescott Point reveals the spread of commerce and industry across the flats. By this time, much of the flats' remaining housing was located east of Robert. The Jewish population was especially large in that part of the flats, accounting for 71 percent of the households in 1915.

Thirty years later, the flats still retained much of their historic character, especially along the Wabasha corridor, as photographs from 1948 and 1954 demonstrate. War surplus items were a hot commodity at this time, and one sign in the 1948 panorama even advertises leftover war buildings for sale. Also visible is the plant operated by the Waterous Company, a manufacturer of pumps and fire hydrants. Waterous later merged with its neighbor, the now defunct American Hoist and Derrick Company (later Amhoist). The 1954 photograph, looking south on Wabasha toward Prescott Point, provides an excellent look at the street's collection of mostly Victorian-era buildings.

Although parts of the flats were cleared as early as the 1920s to make way for a municipal airport (Holman Field) and a barge terminal, large-scale urban renewal did not arrive until the late 1950s. One impetus was the great flood of 1952, then the worst in the city's history. The flood caused $5 million worth of damage and spurred renewal efforts on the flats, especially after the U.S. Army Corps of Engineers built a flood wall. In 1961 the St. Paul Port Authority and the city's Housing and Redevelopment Authority finally began the huge clearance project that would transform the flats from a mixed residential-industrial-commercial area into Riverview Industrial Park.

All told, the agencies cleared more than four hundred acres of land and displaced more than five hundred families still living on the flats, many of them Mexican Americans who had supplanted the earlier Jewish population. Little housing remained on the flats after the work was finished. As part of the renewal project, many of the flats' historic streets were also eliminated—including Chicago, Indiana, Texas, Kentucky, and the biblical duo of Daniel and Moses. A few older warehouse and industrial buildings withstood the onslaught and now provide the flats' only historic architecture.

The 1995 views, from Prescott Point and from near Wabasha and Fillmore, show the results of the Riverview project. All the old Victorians on Wabasha are gone, replaced by a variety of low, modern buildings set amid large lawns. The flats, in other words, now look exactly like a suburban industrial park, which is indeed what they have become.

Still the rich history of the flats is far from over. In the 1990s, more than twenty acres of prime riverfront land on the flats (including the old Amhoist site) was cleared for redevelopment. Since then, there has been talk of building everything from an amphitheater to a major league baseball park on the property. It is thus possible that the flats—long a poor and neglected part of St. Paul—may yet play a significant role in revitalizing the city.

1   4   5 6 7   *1948*

Buildings and Places

1. Wabasha Street Bridge, 1859, 1870s–89; second bridge, Andreas Munster, 1889, 1899–1996; third bridge to open 1997–98
2. Railroad swing bridge (under construction), ca. 1885
3. Farwell, Ozmun, & Kirk Co. warehouse (now various tenants), Water St. and Bidwell St., ca. 1890s
4. J. G. Cherry Co. building (now Wabasha Center), 27–37 Fairfield Ave. E. (today near Wabasha and Fillmore), ca. 1915
5. Waterous Co. plant, 40–80 Fillmore Ave. E., ca. 1917–ca. 60s
6. Chicago and Great Western lift bridge, 1913, 1925
7. Robert Street Bridge (second), 1926 (Toltz, King, and Day), 1990
8. Prescott Point stairs
9. HealthPartners (originally Group Health) medical clinic, Wabasha and Plato, ca. 1980
10. Llewelyn Worldwide Ltd. (originally Coca-Cola bottling plant), Wabasha and Fillmore, Ernest H. Schmidt & Co., 1941

1954

8

8

Reference Notes

Time and Transformation

Montgomery Schuyler, "Glimpses of Western Architecture: St. Paul and Minneapolis," *Harper's Magazine*, Oct. 1891, reprinted in Montgomery Schuyler, *American Architecture and Other Writings*, ed. William H. Jordy and Ralph Coe (Cambridge, Mass.: Harvard University Press, Belknap Press, 1961), 293; Stewart Brand, *How Buildings Learn: What Happens after They're Built* (New York: Viking, 1994), 5.

Minneapolis Downtown

INDUSTRIAL EXPOSITION BUILDING: *Minneapolis Tribune*, Aug. 24, 1886; James Berman, ed., *Saint Anthony Falls Rediscovered* (Minneapolis: Minneapolis Riverfront Development Coordination Board, 1980), 61, 78.

FIRST STREET AND FIRST AVENUE NORTH: Norene Roberts and Joe Roberts, "The Historical Resources of Block 12, Bridge Square, Minneapolis, Minnesota," in *Federal Reserve Bank of Minneapolis, Addendum to Section 106 Documentation*, Apr. 1993; Joseph Stipanovich, *City of Lakes: An Illustrated History of Minneapolis* (Woodland Hills, Calif.: Windsor Publications, 1982), 352; *St. Paul Pioneer Press*, June 21, 1994, p. 1A, June 30, 1994, p. 1B.

GATEWAY: Judith A. Martin and Antony Goddard, *Past Choices/Present Landscapes: The Impact of Urban Renewal on the Twin Cities* (Minneapolis: University of Minnesota, Center for Urban and Regional Affairs, 1989), 57-69; Linda Mack, "Gateways of Change," *Architecture Minnesota*, May-June 1991, p. 36-39, 64-65.

WASHINGTON AVENUE: Calvin F. Schmid, *Social Saga of Two Cities: An Ecological and Statistical Study of Social Trends in Minneapolis and St. Paul* (Minneapolis: Council of Social Agencies, Bureau of Social Research, 1937), 51-52; Lucile M. Kane and John A. Dougherty, "Movie Debut: Films in the Twin Cities, 1894-1909," *Minnesota History* 54 (Winter 1995): 346-47.

NICOLLET AVENUE: *St. Paul and Minneapolis Pioneer Press*, Aug. 26, 1888, p. 1; Paul Larson, "Lost Minnesota,"

Architecture Minnesota, Jan.-Feb. 1990, p. 64; *Saturday Evening Spectator*, July 21, 1886, p. 9, Jan. 15, 1887, p. 1; *St. Paul Pioneer Press*, Apr. 8, 1990, p. 2D.

THIRD STREET: Brand, *How Buildings Learn*, 24-33; *St. Paul Pioneer Press*, Nov. 26, 1882, p. 3; *St. Paul and Minneapolis Pioneer Press*, Apr. 13, 1886, p. 4; *St. Paul Daily Globe*, Apr. 1, 1889, p. 1.

FOURTH STREET: *Saturday Evening Spectator*, Jan. 21, 1888, p. 11; *Minneapolis Golden Jubilee: 1867-1917: A History of Fifty Years of Civic and Commercial Progress* (Minneapolis: [Tribune Co.?], 1917), 121; Jack El-Hai, "Lost Minnesota," *Architecture Minnesota*, July-Aug. 1995, p. 60.

FIFTH STREET: *Minneapolis Tribune*, Jan. 1, 1882, p. 7; *St. Paul Pioneer Press*, Apr. 2, 1989, p. 2D; *St. Paul and Minneapolis Pioneer Press*, Sept. 10, 1882, p. 6.

FIFTH STREET NORTH: Donald R. Torbert, *Significant Architecture in the History of Minneapolis* (Minneapolis: City Planning Commission, 1969), 70-71.

SIXTH STREET NORTH: James A. Roe, "Hay Wagons, New Potatoes and Early Mornings: The Farmers' Markets of Minneapolis," *Hennepin History* (Fall 1990): 4-12; *Minneapolis Journal*, Oct. 9, 1894, p. 2-3; Martin and Goddard, *Past Choices/Present Landscapes*, 33.

SEVENTH STREET: *Minneapolis Journal*, Dec. 12, 1909, pt. 10, special Hotel Radisson sec.; Beatrice Morosco, "Famous Visitors: When Washington Avenue Was the Great White Way," *Hennepin County History* (Summer 1972): 11.

HENNEPIN AVENUE: John R. Borchert, David Gebhard, David Lanegran, and Judith A. Martin, *Legacy of Minneapolis: Preservation amid Change* (Minneapolis: Voyageur Press, 1983), 29, 42; Loring M. Staples, *The West Hotel Story, 1884-1940: Memoirs of Past Splendor* (Minneapolis: Carlson Printing Co., 1979); *St. Paul Pioneer Press and Dispatch*, Nov. 8, 1987, p. 2E; *St. Paul Pioneer Press*, Aug. 29, 1991, p. 10C, Nov. 21, 1993, p. 1B.

EIGHTH STREET: *St. Paul Daily Globe*, Jan. 16, 1888, p. 1; *St. Paul Pioneer Press*, Aug. 13, 1989, p. 7D.

TENTH STREET: Bruce Weir Benidt, *The Library Book: Centennial History of the Minneapolis Public Library* (Minneapolis: Minneapolis Public Library and Information Center, 1984); *St. Paul Pioneer Press*, Apr. 24, 1988, p. 2D,

June 10, 1989, p. 12A.

MARQUETTE AVENUE FROM NINTH STREET: *Minneapolis Tribune*, Sept. 5, 1955; Gael Fashingbauer Cooper, "Whither the Weatherball?" *Mpls-St. Paul*, June 1995, p. 178.

MARQUETTE AVENUE FROM FIFTH STREET: *Western Architect*, May 1907, p. 55, 56, following xxxii; *Minneapolis Journal*, July 9, 1904.

SECOND AVENUE AND FOURTH STREET SOUTH: *Minneapolis Journal*, May 31, 1890, p. 1; *St. Paul and Minneapolis Pioneer Press*, June 1, 1890, p. 7; *Minneapolis Star*, Aug. 11, 1961, p. 11A; Marion D. Shutter, ed., *History of Minneapolis: Gateway to the Northwest* (Chicago and Minneapolis: S. J. Clarke Publishing Co., 1923), 651-54.

SECOND AVENUE SOUTH FROM TENTH STREET: *Foshay Tower: A Business Address of Prestige* (Minneapolis: W. B. Foshay Co., 1929), 3-13; *St. Paul Pioneer Press and Dispatch*, Mar. 8, 1987, p. 2B.

THIRD AVENUE SOUTH FROM TWELFTH STREET: *Lake Area News* (Minneapolis), July 1984, p. 15; *Saturday Evening Spectator*, Sept. 1, 1888, p. 1; *St. Paul Daily Globe*, May 1, 1889, p. 8; *Minneapolis, City of Opportunity: A Century of Progress in the Aquatennial City* (Minneapolis: T. S. Denison and Co., 1956), 161-62; *Star Tribune*, May 10, 1990, p. 4E; *St. Paul Pioneer Press*, May 9, 1990, p. 1D.

PORTLAND AVENUE AND GRANT STREET: Michael Karl Witzel, *The American Gas Station* (Osceola, Wis.: Motorbooks International, 1992), 85-94; Shutter, ed., *History of Minneapolis*, 596.

GRANT STREET: Steve Trimble, *In the Shadow of the City: A History of the Loring Park Neighborhood* (Minneapolis: Minneapolis Community College Foundation, 1989), 30-33, 36-40, 52-55, 79, 102-3; Bill Scott, "A Place to Live: An Architectural History of Loring," in Burt Berlowe et al., *Reflections in Loring Pond: A Minneapolis Neighborhood Examines Its First Century* (Minneapolis: Citizens for a Loring Park Community, 1986), 60-63; *Saturday Evening Spectator*, Jan. 9, 1886, p. 11, Apr. 23, 1887, p. 19.

HARMON PLACE: Trimble, *Shadow of the City*, 47-49, 70-72, 132; John S. Adams and Barbara J. VanDrasek, *Minneapolis-St. Paul: People, Place, and Public Life* (Minneapolis: University of Minnesota Press, 1993), 109.

LORING PARK: Theodore Wirth, *Minneapolis Park System, 1883-1944: Retrospective Glimpses into the History of the Board of Park Commissioners* (Minneapolis: Board of Park Commissioners, 1946), 39, 101-2; Frank W. Wiltberger, "Some Facts and Fancies about Loring Park and the Adjoining Property," *Hennepin County History* (Apr. 1947): 5-6; Garth Rockcastle, "Loring Park: An Enlightened and Romantic Space," in *Reflections in Loring Pond*, 17-26; Trimble, *Shadow of the City*, 25-27, 34-36, 112; *Minneapolis Journal*, Mar. 6, 1933, p. 5.

THE BOTTLENECK: *Minneapolis Journal*, Jan. 28, 1905,

p. 12; *Lake Area News*, Dec. 1983, p. 18; Trimble, *Shadow of the City*, 62-63, 114-16, 134-35.

THIRD STREET SOUTH FROM FOURTEENTH: Judith A. Martin, *Recycling the Central City: The Development of a New Town-In Town* (Minneapolis: University of Minnesota, Center for Urban and Regional Affairs, 1978), 28; Stipanovich, *City of Lakes*, 371.

Minneapolis Neighborhoods

CENTRAL AVENUE: Judith A. Martin and David Lanegran, *Where We Live: The Residential Districts of Minneapolis and Saint Paul* (Minneapolis: University of Minnesota, Center for Urban and Regional Affairs, and University of Minnesota Press, 1983), 16-18.

WEST BROADWAY: Russell L. Olson, *The Electric Railways of Minnesota* (Hopkins, Minn.: Minnesota Transportation Museum, 1976), 19, 31; Borchert, et al., *Legacy of Minneapolis*, 190.

PLYMOUTH AVENUE: Rhoda G. Lewin, "From Ghettos to Neighborhoods: Jewish Immigration in Minneapolis," *Hennepin History* (Winter 1992): 13-27; Willard A. Hutt, "Smoke on Plymouth Avenue," *Hennepin History* (Summer 1992): 25-29.

SIXTH AVENUE NORTH (OLSON HIGHWAY): Jeffrey A. Hess, "Sumner Field Homes: Public Housing in Minnesota before World War II," *Hennepin History* (Winter 1993): 26-35; Martin and Goddard, *Past Choices/Present Landscapes*, 32-41.

PARK AVENUE: *Saturday Evening Spectator*, Jan. 15, 1887, p. 8; *St. Paul and Minneapolis Pioneer Press*, Sept. 10, 1889, p. 6.

EAST LAKE CALHOUN PARKWAY: Stipanovich, *City of Lakes*, 6-7; Wirth, *Minneapolis Park System*, 84, 120.

HENNEPIN AVENUE AT COLFAX AVENUE AND LAKE STREET: David A. Lanegran and Ernest R. Sandeen, *The Lake District of Minneapolis: A History of the Calhoun-Isles Community* (St. Paul: Living Historical Museum, 1979), 41-46; *Lake Area News*, Dec. 1981, p. 5B, 7B, May 1991, p. 28-31.

LAKE STREET AT LYNDALE AVENUE: David Wood, "'Lyndale Corners,' South Minneapolis's First Shopping Area," *Lake Area News*, Aug. 1983, p. 1, 11, 20; Stew Thornley, *On to Nicollet: The Glory and Fame of the Minneapolis Millers* (Minneapolis: Nodin Press, 1988), 19; Lanegran and Sandeen, *Lake District*, 40; Olson, *Electric Railways*, 51.

LAKE STREET AND HIAWATHA AVENUE: Nicholas Westbrook, ed., *A Guide to the Industrial Archeology of the Twin Cities* (St. Paul and Minneapolis: Society for Industrial Archeology, 1983), 92; *St. Paul Pioneer Press*, Dec. 21, 1972, p. 25, Dec. 25, 1972, p. 25.

FRANKLIN AVENUE: *St. Paul Dispatch and St. Paul Pioneer Press Yearbook and Almanac, 1916* (St. Paul: Dispatch Printing Co., 1916), 633; George H. Herrold, "City Planning in St. Paul," *City Planning* 7 (Oct. 1931): 217-24; Thomas W. Balcom, "Mills, Monuments and Malls: A Century of Planning Progress in Downtown Minneapolis," *Hennepin County History* (Spring 1988): 8-14.

CEDAR AVENUE: David Markle, "Dania Hall: History and Prospects," unpublished paper, Jan. 1993, n.p.; Martin, *Recycling the Central City*.

SEVEN CORNERS: Martin, *Recycling the Central City*, 11-24; Martin and Goddard, *Past Choices/Present Landscapes*, 118-23.

St. Paul Downtown

HARRIET ISLAND TOWARD DOWNTOWN: Virginia Brainard Kunz, *The Mississippi and St. Paul: A Short History of the City's 150-Year Love Affair with Its River* (St. Paul: Ramsey County Historical Society, 1987), 28-31; *St. Paul Pioneer Press*, Sept. 13, 1994, p. 1A, Aug. 20, 1995, p. 1B.

WABASHA STREET: *St. Paul Pioneer Press*, Jan. 1, 1891, p. 2; Larry Millett, "Playland," *Architecture Minnesota*, Nov.-Dec. 1995, p. 14-17, 38.

SEVENTH STREET EAST FROM WABASHA: *St. Paul Pioneer Press*, June 4, 1984, p. 1D, Apr. 11, 1993, p. 1E; *St. Paul Pioneer Press and Dispatch*, July 5, 1986, p. 5A; *Capital Centre: A Project for the Central Business District of Downtown St. Paul* ([St. Paul: Metropolitan Improvement Committee, 1962]).

SIXTH STREET: Aaron Isaacs, ed., *Twin City Lines: The 1940s* (St. Paul: Minnesota Transportation Museum, 1995), 4; Edward H. Bennett, William E. Parsons, and George H. Herrold, *Plan of St. Paul: The Capital City of Minnesota* ([St. Paul]: Commissioner of Public Works, 1922).

CEDAR STREET: *St. Paul Daily Globe*, May 1, 1887, p. 1; Eileen Michels, "Landscape of Government," in *Saint Paul Omnibus: Images of the Changing City*, ed. Bonnie Richter (St. Paul: Old Town Restorations, Inc., 1979), 26-28; *Capital Centre*.

ST. PETER, WASHINGTON, AND MARKET STREETS: *St. Paul Dispatch*, Sept. 23, 1959, p. 6; Eileen Michels, with a chapter by Nate J. Bomberg, *A Landmark Reclaimed* (St. Paul: Minnesota Landmarks, 1977).

FIFTH STREET: *The Auditorium at St. Paul, Reed & Stem, Architects* (St. Paul: Midway Publishing Co., [1910?]), n.p.; *Western Architect* 16, no. 5 (Nov. 1910): [125].

ROBERT STREET: George H. Herrold, "The Necessity for Coordinated Planning," *Civil Engineering* 1 (Dec. 1931): 1329; Herrold, "City Planning in St. Paul," 220; Larry Millett, *Lost Twin Cities* (St. Paul: Minnesota Historical Society Press, 1992), 170-71, 174-75; *St. Paul Pioneer Press*, July 24, 1989, p. 9A.

THIRD STREET: Herrold, "Necessity," 1327-28; Gareth Hiebert, *Saint Paul Is My Beat* (St. Paul: North Central Publishing Co., 1958), 46; Thomas J. Kelley, "A Case History of Government in Action: The Newly Restored, Newly Renovated City Hall-County Courthouse," *Ramsey County History* 28, no. 3 (Fall 1993): 5; Herrold, "City Planning in St. Paul," 220.

FOURTH STREET: *St. Paul Dispatch*, Jan. 12, 1876, p. 4; Richard Moe, *The Last Full Measure: The Life and Death of the First Minnesota Volunteers* (New York: Henry Holt and Co., 1993), 304; Olson, *Electric Railways*, 34-35.

SEVENTH STREET EAST FROM SIBLEY STREET: Millett, *Lost Twin Cities*, 17-21; Herrold, "Necessity," 1333.

SEVENTH STREET EAST FROM ROSABEL STREET: *St. Paul and Minneapolis Pioneer Press*, Dec. 6, 1884, p. 8; Virginia Brainard Kunz, *St. Paul: Saga of an American City* (Woodland Hills, Calif.: Windsor Publications, Inc., 1977), 54.

GREAT NORTHERN FREIGHT TERMINAL: *A Century of Service to God and Man: Brief History of the Church of Saint Mary of St. Paul, Minnesota, 1867-1967* ([St. Paul: St. Mary's Church, 1967]); Patricia Ann Murphy, "The Early Career of Cass Gilbert: 1878-1895" (Master's thesis, University of Virginia, 1979), 56.

UNION DEPOT RAIL YARDS: Kunz, *St. Paul*, 143-44; Westbrook, ed., *Industrial Archeology*, 82.

DAYTON'S BLUFF: Josiah B. Chaney, "Early Bridges and Changes of the Land and Water Surface in the City of St. Paul," *Collections of the Minnesota Historical Society* 12 (1905-08): 136-37; *St. Paul Pioneer Press*, July 6, 1993, p. 1B.

MERRIAM'S HILL: E. V. Smalley, "St. Paul," *Northwest Magazine*, Apr. 1886, p. 12; *St. Paul Pioneer Press*, Aug. 21, 1887, p. 10, Oct. 7, 1888, p. 17; Henry A. Castle, *History of St. Paul and Vicinity: A Chronicle of Progress . . .* (Chicago and New York: Lewis Publishing Co., 1912), 2:703-4; *St. Paul Dispatch*, Jan. 15, 1964, p. 31.

WABASHA STREET NORTH FROM THIRTEENTH STREET: Isaacs, ed., *Twin City Lines*, 4, 7; Gary Phelps, *History of the Minnesota State Capitol Area* (St. Paul: Capitol Area Architectural and Planning Board, 1985), 11-18, 26-38.

CEDAR STREET FROM EAST CAPITOL PLAZA: *St. Paul Dispatch*, May 11, 1948, p. 16, Nov. 7, 1958, p. 20; Castle, *St. Paul and Vicinity*, 2:906; *St. Paul Pioneer Press*, Sept. 5, 1990, p. 1B.

TWELFTH STREET: Westbrook, ed., *Industrial Archeology*, 126-27; J. Fletcher Williams, *A History of the City of Saint Paul to 1875* (St. Paul: Minnesota Historical Society, 1876, Borealis Books, 1983), 166; *St. Paul Pioneer Press*, May 15, 1993, p. 4D.

FIFTH STREET WEST TOWARD THIRD STREET: *St. Paul and Minneapolis Pioneer Press*, Aug. 28, 1887, p. 13; Eric C. Hanson, *The Cathedral of St. Paul: An Architectural Biography* (St. Paul: Cathedral of St. Paul, 1990).

SEVEN CORNERS: *St. Paul and Minneapolis Pioneer Press*, June 17, 1888, p. 14; *St. Paul Pioneer Press*, Apr. 8, 1962, Sunday Pictorial Magazine, p. 18-19, Dec. 14, 1992, p. 1B; Hiebert, *St. Paul Is My Beat*, 116; *St. Paul Pioneer and Democrat*, Nov. 25, 1860, p. 1; *St. Paul Dispatch*, Jan. 14, 1981, p. 14D.

MAIN STREET: Donald Empson, *The Street Where You Live: A Guide to the Street Names of St. Paul* (St. Paul: Witsend Press, 1975), 95; "St. Paul's Growth in 1888," *Northwest Magazine*, Feb. 1889, p. 9; William B. Hennessey, *Past and Present of St. Paul, Minnesota* (Chicago: S. J. Clarke Publishing Co., 1906), 652-53.

PLEASANT AVENUE: *St. Paul and Minneapolis Pioneer Press*, Sept. 2, 1888, p. 14; *St. Paul Daily Globe*, Feb. 11, 1889, p. 1; *St. Paul Pioneer Press*, Jan. 1, 1939, p. 3, Oct. 7, 1990, p. 1A.

SUMMIT AND DAYTON AVENUES: *St. Paul and Minneapolis Pioneer Press*, Dec. 3, 1882, p. 3; Paul Clifford Larson, "Lost Minnesota," *Architecture Minnesota*, May-June 1989, p. 114; Ernest R. Sandeen, *St. Paul's Historic Summit Avenue* (St. Paul: Living Historical Museum, Macalester College, 1978), 22, 42; *Inland Architect*, July 1885, p. 97-98; Olson, *Electric Railways*, 41-43.

SUMMIT AVENUE AND SIXTH STREET: *St. Paul Pioneer Press*, Mar. 1, 1895, p. 5; *St. Paul Dispatch*, Sept. 2, 1920, city progress sec., p. 16; Virginia McAlester and Lee McAlester, *A Field Guide to American Houses* (New York: Alfred A. Knopf, 1984), 235-37.

HIGH BRIDGE: Susan Hodapp, *St. Paul's High Bridge, 1889-1985: A Photo-Essay of the History of a St. Paul Landmark* (St. Paul: Minnesota Department of Transportation, 1985), 25-29; *Discover St. Paul: A Short History of Seven St. Paul Neighborhoods* (St. Paul: Ramsey County Historical Society, 1979), 35.

St. Paul Neighborhoods

PAYNE AVENUE: *Discover St. Paul*, 45-50; David Lanegran, "Building the City," in Richter, ed., *Saint Paul Omnibus*, 13-14; Patricia A. Murphy and Susan W. Granger, *Historic Sites Survey of St. Paul and Ramsey County, 1980-1983: Final Report* (St. Paul: St. Paul Heritage Preservation Commission and Ramsey County Historical Society, 1983), 47-55.

WELLS STREET: Information on date of wall from St. Paul city records provided by James Sazevich; *Saint Paul Public Schools: A Century of Service, 1856-1956* (St. Paul: St. Paul Public Schools, 1956), n.p.

ARCADE STREET: James B. Bell, "The Story of the Seeger Refrigerator Company," *Ramsey County History* 30, no. 1 (Spring 1995): 4-13; *St. Paul Pioneer Press*, June 17, 1994, p. 1E.

UNIVERSITY AVENUE AT RICE STREET: Olson, *Electric Railways*, 37; Martin and Goddard, *Past Choices/Present Landscapes*, 26-30.

UNIVERSITY AVENUE NEAR SNELLING AVENUE: *St. Paul Pioneer Press*, Apr. 3, 1921, Montgomery Ward & Co. sec., p. 1-12, Apr. 2, 1995, p. 1G, Jan. 8, 1996, p. 1A; Olson, *Electric Railways*, 255-56.

RAYMOND AVENUE: David A. Lanegran with Judith Frost Flinn, *St. Anthony Park: Portrait of a Community* (St. Paul: District 12 Community Council and St. Anthony Park Assn., 1987), 96, 101-5; *St. Paul Plan for Fire Stations, Community Plan Report No. 11* (St. Paul: City Planning Board, 1961), 9.

SELBY AVENUE: *St. Paul Pioneer Press*, Feb. 28, 1993, p. 1G; Martin and Goddard, *Past Choices/Present Landscapes*, 101-10.

HIGH BRIDGE ACROSS UPPER LEVEE FLATS: *St. Paul Daily Globe*, June 8, 1889, p. 2; *St. Paul Dispatch*, June 9, 1960, p. 23.

PRESCOTT POINT ACROSS WEST SIDE FLATS: Martin and Goddard, *Past Choices/Present Landscapes*, 42-48; Demian J. Hess and Jeffrey A. Hess, "Historic American Engineering Record, Wabasha Street Bridge," Dec. 1993, p. 4-16; "West St. Paul," *Northwest Magazine*, Nov. 1886, p. 10-24; William Hoffman, *Those Were the Days* (Minneapolis: T. S. Denison and Co., 1957), 20; Westbrook, ed., *Industrial Archeology*, 126.

Index

Picture Credits

The photographs used in this book appear through the courtesy of the institutions listed below. The name of the photographer, when known, is given in parentheses, as is additional information about the source of the item. All new photographs are by Jerry Mathiason.

Minnesota Historical Society collections, St. Paul pages 6, 7, 18 (Norton and Peel), 20, 21 (top), 22 (A. D. Roth), 24 (Norton and Peel), 29 (top; A. D. Roth), 30 (Norton and Peel), 32 (Lee Brothers), 33 (Norton and Peel), 36 (A. D. Roth), 38, 39, 40 (Norton and Peel), 42 (Luxton), 43, 44, 46 (Norton and Peel), 48 (Norton and Peel), 50 (Sweet), 52, 54, 56 (Norton and Peel), 58, 61 (top), 62 (Lee Brothers), 66 (Minneapolis Star-Journal), 67 (bottom; Philip C. Dittes, St. Paul), 68, 74 (Hibbard), 75 (top), 76, 78, 82, 86, 88 (Northern Pacific Railroad Public Relations/Adv. and Publicity Dept. Records), 90, 92 (Norton and Peel), 93 (top), 94, 95 (top), 96, 98, 104 (Gibson), 106, 107 (top), 108, 110, 111 (top; Kenneth M. Wright, St. Paul), 112 (Northwestern Photographic Studio, Inc., St. Paul), 116 (Gibson), 118 (Gibson), 124 (C. P. Gibson), 126, 134, 136 (top), 136 (bottom; C. P. Gibson), 140, 141 (top), 142, 144, 146, 150, 152 (C. P. Gibson), 155 (bottom), 156, 159 (top), 160, 161 (bottom; C. P. Gibson), 162 (Gibson), 164 (Gibson), 170, 172, 176, 178, 182, 184 (St. Paul Dispatch-Pioneer Press), 186 (Ingersoll, St. Paul), 187 (bottom), 188 (St. Paul Dispatch-Pioneer Press), 189 (Norton and Peel)

Minneapolis Public Library, Minneapolis Collection pages 14, 16, 26, 28, 34, 60, 64, 80, 84 (Sweet)

St. Paul Pioneer Press pages 114, 128, 130, 138, 148, 154, 155 (top and middle)

Minnesota Transportation Museum pages 120 (both), 122 (both)

Ramsey County Historical Society pages 132, 174, 180, 183 (top)

Private Collection page 143 (top)